The GHOST *of Eternal*
POLYGAMY

The GHOST *of Eternal* POLYGAMY

Haunting the Hearts and Heaven of Mormon Women and Men

CAROL LYNN PEARSON

Pivot Point Books
ISBN-13: 978-0997458206
ISBN-10: 0997458208

Library of Congress Control Number: 2016907928

Design and typesetting by John Hamer
Cover concept by Michele Encisco Bendall

Sincere appreciation to:

- Greg Prince for his invaluable assistance with the online survey and for giving me the courage to believe I could make my own small adjustment to the course of history

- The more than 8,000 women and men who trusted me enough to take the survey and share stories of their most private pain

- My sister, Marie Wright Cheever, for standing witness via the telephone, listening to yet another, and yet another, heart-breaking story as I spent a summer studying the results of the survey

- Shauna Summers for enthusiasm, contacts, and for being first in the publishing world to say, "This is going to be a really terrific and important book"

- Dan Wotherspoon for his good eye as editor and his good heart as friend

- John Hamer for his exceptional creativity in designing the cover and the interior of the book

- Michele Encisco Bendall, for the concept of the book cover, and for being my social media guru and dear friend

- Lindsay Hansen Park for inspiration, for spending a year swimming in the history of Mormon polygamy and doing extraordinary work toward the well-being of both fundamentalist and LDS women and men

- Several church leaders whose confidence in the importance of this book has meant the world to me

- Rozan, Kathleen, Christy, Judy, and Susan, uppity Mormon sisters who have met in my home monthly for more than twenty years, helping each other stay sane, becoming our own authority, and getting very clear on what has to be swept out the door of our spiritual homes. "Don't you think," said naïve and hopeful Christy in 1995, "if they knew how bad polygamy hurts us, they would get rid of it? We need to just write and tell them!"

To the Author from Early Readers:

When my husband finished reading *The Ghost of Eternal Polygamy*, he came to me and asked through his tears, "Have you felt this way in our marriage?" I said that I had. He held me, and we cried together, grieved at the unnecessary pain that had disrupted the strong love and trust that we have for each other, and so relieved that we will never have to feel that pain again. Sometimes now I snuggle up to him in bed and whisper, *"You are mine, only mine!"* I could never say that before.

Not being a woman, I've had little trouble simply ignoring polygamy, past and future—but no more. I just finished reading your wonderful book at a single sitting and I'll never be the same. It is your crowning masterpiece. What a combination of faith, storytelling, honesty, and positivity. You say some hard things in a soft and loving way. I think a hundred years from now people will look back on this as the major contribution that it is, moving us all toward being ONE. The entire book—but especially the ending—is strong, uniting, and uplifting.

I am speechless. I just finished reading *The Ghost of Eternal Polygamy*, and even though my husband had finished it, I still had to read out loud to him, twenty times at least, some of the stories. This is powerful stuff, and you are one of the bravest women I have ever known. You're a healer once again!

Oh, so wonderful! What surpasses *heroic*? I concluded the reading with a strengthened faith and sense of understanding and empathy. I am a better man as well. May you be blessed for such caring work—and may we be blessed as well.

I'm gobsmacked! And only halfway through the book. As a Catholic, it's hard for me to take seriously some of the things that are believed by those whose stories you tell. But it is powerful and fascinating. And the fact that some of it is your own family history gives it even more power. Can't wait to read more!

I am deeply grateful that you are strong enough to state the issues for the rest of us to think about. You have done so with love, brilliance, and compassion. I am impressed with the way you can love Joseph and still reject polygamy. Thank you for that example.

As an attorney, I think you have skillfully and masterfully made your case, brick by brick, until by the end there is no question but that we need to do immediately what you urge. Bless you for this work of art.

Even though I'm not a Mormon, I sometimes found myself in tears to be reading something so fascinating and profound and moving. I couldn't put it down.

Wow! And Wow! I just finished reading and then rereading *The Ghost of Eternal Polygamy*. It is incredible. I love you for having the talent and the courage to so beautifully put into words all the thoughts and emotions regarding polygamy that have haunted me all these years. I felt many emotions as I read the stories that were told so vividly I felt I was there watching them—anger, sadness, pain, embarrassment, shame, discouragement and, finally, hope—not just *endure to the end*, but hope!

Reading *The Ghost of Eternal Polygamy* has been so good for my soul. Thank you! I was afraid to begin the book, to be honest, because I was nervous about what sorts of feelings and anxieties it would stir up. I am grateful now for every sentence and for every thought.

I just finished the book and I am in tears, overwhelmed with gratitude. My heart is broken with all the stories, yet comforted to know that I am not alone in the pain. Your words give me hope. I have not been an active member of the church for several years, mainly due to my struggle with polygamy and the current church policies concerning women and our LGBT brothers and sisters. Reading your book, especially the last couple of chapters, almost makes me want to believe, to hope that the church of my childhood could be a safe place again.

The justification of discrimination against women and girls
on grounds of religion or tradition,
as if it were prescribed by a Higher Authority, is unacceptable.

—Nelson Mandela and "The Elders"

One of the grand fundamental principles of Mormonism
is to receive truth,
let it come from whence it may.

—Joseph Smith, the Mormon Prophet

Contents

Mormon Terminology

Ward—a geographical congregation of the church, composed of several hundred members, equivalent to a parish

Bishop—the presiding officer and spiritual leader of a ward, equivalent to a pastor, serves with two counselors

Stake—a geographical unit of the church, composed of a number of wards

Stake President—the presiding officer and spiritual leader of a stake, serves with two counselors

Auxiliaries—organizations overseen by bishop: Relief Society (women), Young Women, Young Men, Primary (children), Sunday School

Relief Society—organization for all adult Mormon women, focused on service and learning

Visiting teachers—women who are assigned to pay a monthly visit to several other women in the ward, giving an inspirational message and seeing if there are needs that could be addressed

Prophet—the one man who is head of the church: president, prophet, seer and revelator

General Authority—a member of the highest levels of leadership in the church (First Presidency, Quorum of the Twelve Apostles, Quorums of the Seventy) with church-wide authority

Temple—building designated for special ordinances and rituals, available only to those holding a "recommend" of worthiness from the bishop and stake president or their counselors

Sealing—a priesthood ordinance whereby husbands and wives are married for eternity, and parents and children, ancestors and progeny, are bound together in eternal family relationships

Priesthood—the power and authority given to men to act in the name of God

Celestial kingdom—the highest degree of heaven, above the terrestrial and telestial kingdoms

Exaltation—to live in God's presence and continue eternally as families

Doctrine and Covenants (D&C)—a book of LDS scripture, revelations received by the Prophet Joseph Smith with some additions by his successors

D&C Section 132—the revelation that deals with the eternal nature of the marriage covenant, specifically plural marriage

Introduction

MAYBE IT'S BECAUSE my magnolia tree is in full pink and purple bloom as I look out the window of my second story home office that I feel so ready to begin this book. Or maybe it's because this is one of those challenging, thrilling projects that you know will be life-changing. It's a good view out my window. I feel like I'm in a treetop. I light my writing candle and the view gets even better. I glance at the small poster on my wall, an inspiring quote by C.S. Lewis:

> Many things have gone wrong
> with this world
> that God made
> and
> God insists
> and insists very loudly
> on our putting them right again.

There are wrongs to be righted. And yet—"All is well." My pioneer Mormon ancestors sang that stirring song as step by difficult step they crossed the plains to Utah. Is it possible all can be well at the same time that there are things that must be put right? I'm a Libra—on the one hand there's this, on the other hand there's that—and so I can hold both of those thoughts at the same time. It means that we haven't arrived yet, but that we have everything we need to get there, to create "a new heaven and a new earth." It is with these balancing Libra hands that I will write this book—there is so much pain but there is so much promise. It all works because we are forever pioneers.

I'M TOLD THAT I am now one of the "wise-woman elders" of our tribe. In my tribe we don't pay much attention to our wise-woman elders. Our male Elders own the talking stick and occasionally pass it to women, young or old. And so I have learned to make a place for myself and to take that place. My business is to tell the stories. As a fourth-generation actively participating Mormon who has for fifty years written about the joys and failures of our community, about women, men, marriage, love, and truth, I believe it is time to finally tell some of the hardest stories. There is unreasonable pain within the hearts and the homes of many faithful Mormon people, and attention must be paid.

This work will not be labor. Telling these stories will require time and care, but in a way it will be as easy as letting birds out of a cage. Thoughts are things and words have wings. These stories have long been consigned to small spaces, cramped and whispering places, and I smile as I free them. They will unfurl their wings and fly and alight where they will be noticed, homing pigeons that have never had a home, carrying scrawled messages on notes that say, "*...please help.*"

JUST LAST SUNDAY in Relief Society—that's the name of the women's organization in the Mormon Church—our lesson was on developing empathy through knowing one another's stories. The lesson was given by our president Emily, a smart and delightful woman, who began with a story about how sometimes when she is in traffic, anxious because she is late, irate at whatever has caused this mess, she suddenly comes upon the scene of an accident complete with emergency vehicles. "I quickly find myself praying for whoever was in that car and my anger is gone," she said. During our discussion, I contributed a similar story and added, "An old Jewish saying that I love is—'An enemy is someone whose story you do not know.'" That's how important it is to tell our own stories, to reverently tell the stories of others. And to listen.

I'm not angry this morning. I have been. Seeing preventable pain, mine and others, makes me angry. But I know that anger is good only as a fueling station, never as a destination. I have used anger before to move me to good places, and I will do it again. You will read in this book some happy things, but mostly hard things, sad things, disturbing things. You will see open wounds. But the good news is that hands are at the ready to assist in the healing.

My small part in the work of helping to put things right in this world that God made is clear to me. Along with so many other women and men of all cultures, nations, and religions, I have a calling to help the human family cross the plains of Patriarchy and enter the land of Partnership. This pioneering work I was born to. It was written in my bones and rattled around in my head before I even had words. Really, maybe it's because I had such a good sleep last night and my magnolia tree is in full bloom, but as I sat down to this desk I thought—why should I be resentful that prior generations have not finished the job? Everyone needs good work to do. This morning I feel really grateful that so much territory has already been traveled.

I am so grateful that my work is not trying to convince the Parliament in Great Britain to end the slave trade. I'm so glad my work is not trying to stop the burning of witches during the Inquisition in Europe—or debating Augustine over whether or not women have souls—or going on a hunger strike in a brutal prison with Alice Paul and other suffragists demanding the vote in America. Vast territory in that long walk for the dignity and equality of women has been crossed, and I am so grateful. And yet, we live in a world in which, according to a United Nations report:

- Between 113 and 200 million women are missing worldwide because of infanticide or girls not getting the same food or attention to their health that boys get.

- The number of girls and women forced or sold into prostitution is between one and four million per year.

- Globally, women between the age of fifteen and forty-four are more likely to be maimed or die as a result of male violence than through cancer, malaria, traffic accidents or war combined.

- More than two million girls are genitally mutilated each year.

- Systematic rape is used as a weapon of terror in many of the world's conflicts. It is estimated that between 250,000 and 500,000 women in Rwanda were raped during the 1994 genocide.

- Many of these atrocities are influenced by a reading of religion that makes maleness supreme.

BUT THE WORK accelerates. Everywhere abuses are being addressed. The move toward partnership is happening worldwide, exploding the architecture of suppression that was solid for centuries, creating mischief in systems that have been built on the backs of women. When women stand straight things fall and break. The impulse toward partnership is an impulse that will not be stopped because it is a godly impulse.

The corner of God's world that I have been called to live in and work in is a very good place—in the United States of America—in the twenty-first century—and with one of God's favorite people, the Latter-day Saints, the Mormons. Well, it's okay for every people to consider themselves "a favorite" with God as long as we don't take it too seriously and know deep down that all people are God's favorite. God is indiscriminate like that, but also smart like the gift giver on Valentine's Day who knows the beloved needs to feel special, unique even.

In my experience, the Mormon Church is a rich field that offers a nourishing harvest to both women and men. But still there are things here that pollute and poison. We Mormons have inherited from centuries past the same male-centric landscape that most everyone else has. We breathe the same male-centric air. We have the same male-centric scriptures (plus some new ones). We share the same male-centric vision of how things work—maleness is the center of the universe and femaleness orbits around it. Patriarchy is the clothing that we all put on, no matter that it does not fit us. And patriarchy is the food that we eat, no matter that it does not sustain us. We Mormons are definitely patriarchal.

The church—the steeple—the doors—the people. Down at the bottom is where the real church exists. I don't think you can find a better people than the Mormons. And frankly I don't think there's a patriarchy better suited to loading the wagon and crossing the plains toward partnership than my own, and I say that even after examining all evidence to the contrary. I believe that "the field is white" already for partnership. Almost all the men I know—the men in my own extended family—the men in my circle of friendship and of work—the men in leadership positions in my local church experience—I find to be men of integrity, men who are becoming conscious of harmful gender issues, men who are ready to be part of the shift in consciousness necessary to travel toward partnership. And I believe that many Mormon women—even those who have chosen very traditional roles and don't ask many questions—have an uneasy feeling that when women's minds and hearts and voices are peripheral and not central, everyone loses. A prominent non-LDS historian, Wallace Stegner, wrote how deeply he admired the devotion and heroism of the Mormon pioneers. "Especially their women. Their women were incredible." They still are. I watch "conservative" Mormon women sharing their gifts of steadfastness, service, creativity—and I honor them. I watch "progressive" Mormon women sharing their gifts of inquiry, innovation, essential discomfort—and I honor them. The women I attend church with in my local ward are remarkable.

WE MORMONS BELIEVE we are creating Zion. I know that we're just a small corner in God's vast Zion, but if God's eye is on the sparrow surely it is on our little Mormon Zion. I love to say the word "Zion."

The Kabbalah says that Zion and the Holy of Holies are the same. If Zion is holy it must be whole, and if it is whole it must be male and female together, a place of partnership where we can sing the songs of Zion in both treble and bass.

And so we do the work of Zion. I get up in the morning and work my fingers on my little keyboard in my little spot in the little Mormon corner of a Zion that slowly, slowly rises like a sun, coming into focus through the mists of history and misunderstanding.

There are many things that help speed our journey to a Partnership Zion. Our Mormon wagon is full of intelligence, hard work, ingenuity, determination, faith, kindness, and service. But there is one particular thing on board that drags us down. It weighs nothing, but is heavy as a broken heart. We carry a peculiar burden, an extra layer of male entitlement and female impediment that no other religious body in the Judeo-Christian tradition has to carry: a very distressing and complicated past and present and future with God-ordained polygamy.

For close to 200 years, polygamy has been an extraordinarily troublesome subject in Mormondom. Some Mormons today, women and men, view plural marriage as a blessing that we will someday understand. For others it is just a bother, embarrassing and annoying and not to be taken very seriously. But for still others—a great many, I think—it is a blight, rather like the crickets that destroy a crop. These are the people I feel called to serve, and I have never had a calling that I honor more deeply.

IN OCTOBER OF 2014, headlines around the world told of the Mormon Church officially acknowledging that its founding prophet, Joseph Smith, had taken between thirty and forty wives, many of them already married to other men, and one as young as fourteen. The practice was commanded by God, said the statement, and the practice was ended by God in 1890.

"Polygamy?" says the church. "We gave that up long ago."

But on this we do not tell the truth; we do not even tell it slant. We tell it veiled and hope the story will not be examined closely. Any member of the LDS Church today that enters the practice of polygamy is immediately excommunicated. But polygamy itself has never been excommunicated. It is still a member in good standing, waiting on the other side to greet us in heaven and causing large injury here on earth. "Polygamy delayed" is still polygamy. In our church, headquartered in Salt Lake City—not the fundamentalist and often violent or bizarre break-off groups such as the one made infamous by Warren Jeffs—but the LDS Church of the Tabernacle Choir, Mitt Romney, and Donny and Marie Osmond—the church that I attend weekly—polygamy is not an artifact in a museum. It is alive and unwell, a Ghost that has a dark life of its own—hiding in the recesses of the Mormon psyche, inflicting profound pain and fear, assuring women that we are still objects, damaging or destroying marriages, bringing chaos to family relationships, leading many to lose faith in our church and in God. In spite of its obvious damage, the Ghost is given an honored place at the family table.

Fundamental to Mormon doctrine is that in order to be "exalted," allowed to live eternally in God's highest kingdom, one must be married, and that family relationships can continue after death if they are "sealed" by priesthood authority. This unequivocal doctrine, combined with current "polygamy delayed" practices and teachings, results in these facts and feelings:

- A Mormon man, widowed or divorced, can sequentially have sealed to him a number of wives, secure in the promise that they will be his in eternity. Of this, one woman wrote me: *"I feel incredible dread of an eternity in which I am assured I will have to live as a plural wife. This sounds like hell to me."*

- A Mormon widow who has already been sealed in eternal marriage to her first husband is generally viewed by men as undateable and often feels like a pariah. Wrote one: *"A nice Mormon guy hung up the phone when he found I was a sealed widow. He said he was looking for his Eternal Companion and*

I wasn't it. He said, 'Who wants to love someone and then lose them?' "

- When a woman is sealed to her husband and is later widowed or divorced, if she remarries and has children with her new husband (and has not been allowed to or has not wanted to cancel that sealing), those children are automatically sealed to the first husband and not to their biological father. *"My step-dad raised me and my sister and my two half-brothers. I love him deeply and consider him my father, but I'm told that my step-dad will have to marry someone else in heaven after he dies because my mom and all of us kids will 'belong' to her first husband. This almost made my step-dad back out on the day of their wedding. I no longer believe this terrible doctrine has anything to do with God."*

- Many women suffer excruciating pain under the long-taught assumption that if they and their husband are sufficiently righteous they will be expected to live polygamy in the celestial kingdom. Some men seem to look forward to that and are oblivious to the deep distress this brings to their wives. *"Eternal polygamy is a searingly painful topic for all Mormon women of my acquaintance—at least, those who have seriously contemplated it. I find it unconscionable and incompatible in every way with the God I worship."*

No, polygamy is not a thing of the past for many Mormons. The Ghost creates tension in their everyday lives, compromising the way they see the one in the mirror, the one on the other side of the bed, and the One they are told thought this all up in the first place.

IN MARCH OF 2014, I reached out to Mormons and former Mormons via social media, asking them to take a survey about their opinions and feelings regarding the LDS concept of eternal polygamy and the inequality of the sealing practices. On the first day more than 2400 people took the survey. Four weeks later more than 8000 had responded. Since the respondents were self-selected, the sample is not necessarily representative of the population of members and former members of the LDS Church. In this particular survey 70 percent of the respondents were female, 30 percent male. 76 percent were married. 91 percent were currently members of the church, while 9 percent were former members. 51 percent of the members were "very active" and 16 percent "somewhat active." 93 percent of the "very active" held current temple recommends. 58 percent reported feelings of sadness or anger regarding the thought of eternal polygamy and the sealing policies. Fewer than 10 percent reported feeling positive emotions on these issues.

Hours after the survey went out, a woman on the East Coast sent me an email. "*Thank you* does not even begin to encompass my gratitude. To have someone I respect so much tackling this issue brings me a lot of comfort." Later in the day I received her story.

> In 2003, I married my husband in the Boston Temple. At the time I was a senior at BYU and my husband was freshly back from his mission to England. I consider myself a very normal, faithful, and mainstream member of the church in a very happy marriage. But after the birth of the last of our three children in 2010, I began to experience an inordinate fear of my own death.
>
> It was always there, that terrible anxiety. As I sifted through my fears, I came to realize the only reason for this terror is because I know that if I die, especially young, my husband will surely remarry and be sealed to another woman, and I will then face an eternity of polygamy. It's that simple. And that fear has developed to the point that I now experience a form of hypochondria.
>
> I have been to an anxiety specialist, but because the doctrine of the church hasn't changed, there's nothing she could do for me. I've been to my doctor nearly every month in the last year, complaining about some symptom or another—because, surely, if we catch the cancer early, I won't die and my husband won't get remarried and I won't have to live polygamy for ever and ever and ever. It's simple. And real. It's my painful truth.
>
> I pray. I fast. I seek peace from my Father in Heaven, but the peace doesn't come. I want to feel like an equal in my eternal marriage. I want to feel the assurance from God that my happiness, both now and eternally, is important to him. But polygamy in the next life seems like a punishment, not eternal glory.

At the end of the survey I specifically asked for stories, all anonymous. I sat week after week, riveted as I read the thousands of stories and comments, categorizing them and watching themes develop. About 15 percent of the stories went into my "at peace with polygamy" category, saying essentially, "God's laws are higher than man's…Polygamy is essential in achieving the highest kingdom… Just trust…God is loving and all will work out." But 85 percent of the stories expressed sadness, confusion, pain. Sometimes as I would read, my nervous system reported *emergency!*—and my hand wanted to reach for the telephone. *Who can I call? Something must be done!* And so I would call my sister Marie in Southern California. Once, four times in one day. "Can you bear hearing another one?" I needed to have a witness. I needed to hear another human making those little sounds of sadness, of disbelief.

Soon I realized that something sacred was going on. Wounded members of my tribe, my family, my people, were handing messages to a wise-woman elder in the hope that she would find a way to let their words be heard: "…*please help*."

I APPRECIATE A bit of wisdom that says: Life works best when we look at everything as being either "My business"—"Your business"— or "God's business."

My business is to tell the stories—the private and painful stories I have been given permission to share, my own personal and family stories, stories from history that tell of plural marriage in nineteenth-century Mormondom, and stories of the ongoing conflict the subject generates today.

Your business may be to read the stories, to think about them, perhaps to share them.

And God's business? To do what God does constantly—to shine on the world and on each one of us with heaven's best gift—a love that leads us out of darkness and gives us enough light to see and enjoy all the things that are true and fine, and also to have the courage to see the things that have gone wrong so we can put them right again.

Stories can conquer fear, you know. They can make the heart bigger.

—Ben Okri

-1-
My Story: This is What God Has in Store for Me?

I CAN REMEMBER the moment I first learned about eternal polygamy almost as clearly as the moment I learned of the assassination of President Kennedy. It was 1956, and I was a junior at Brigham Young University High School in Provo, Utah, where every day we spent an hour of class time in religious study, a course we called "seminary." I remember where I was sitting in the room. I remember the blackboard behind Brother Anderson, our much-loved teacher. This day he wore a light grey suit and a blue tie. I don't remember what the lesson was, possibly the importance of our remaining virtuous and being careful whom and how we dated. But I clearly remember how he said in a very serious tone, "Students, I am going to tell you now something that is deeply important and very tender to me personally."

I perked up and listened. I wanted to learn everything I could that was deeply important.

"My dear wife, a wonderful woman, died some years ago. Later I met and married the woman who is my wife today, also a wonderful woman. She is sealed to me in the temple by the authority of the holy priesthood, as was my first wife. I love them both. Dear young brothers and sisters, I bear you my testimony that in the eternities I will claim both of these women as my wives, and that we will live together forever. And further I bear you my testimony that similarly our Father in Heaven has many wives, our Mothers in Heaven. The doctrine that we call plural marriage, restored by the Prophet Joseph Smith in these latter days, is an essential part of the gospel and is the way the heavens are organized and eternal life is extended.

"I know this may sound strange to you today, especially to you young women. But I promise you that as you live the gospel, as you grow in unselfishness, as you become more pure, you will realize the beauty of this principle, and you will yearn to live it. We are not allowed to live it today, but if we are righteous we will be called to live it in the eternities. This is my testimony to you today. I know that what I have said is true."

I REMEMBER WALKING the six blocks from school to my home, brown leaves crunching on the sidewalk, a heavy sweater pulled tight around me. There was something new in my chest that I had never felt before, something very cold and very confusing. Maybe most of the kids in that seminary class didn't pay much attention to what we had just heard. Or didn't care. I paid attention. And I cared. And I believed. There was no young Mormon girl more devoted to being righteous than I was.

The words I had heard went round and round in my head. *This is what God has in store for me? The God who created me, who loves me? This is how heaven works? I'll be one of many wives forever?*

I was sixteen, very aware that I was developing into a woman, dreaming about being loved, being kissed, being married, very aware of where in the room the boy I had a crush on was sitting. And now—*this!* I must have known about polygamy of long ago, way back in the days of the pioneers, but I didn't know about polygamy as our eternal destiny—forever and ever! It had to be true. My seminary teacher had borne his testimony to us. For the first time in my life, the ground split and there was a frightening divide between me and God, between me and his church.

I would not have been able to articulate it at that time, but I had begun a painful journey toward an impossible goal, a journey that lasted a long time: how to love a God who hurts you.

MY MORMON CHILDHOOD was a good one. I was not by nature an especially happy child. I am an introvert and have always bent toward melancholy. My parents were hard-working, caring but stoic. Life was serious business and it was a good thing we had the church. We knew that if we held to the iron rod, the word of God, it would guide us safely through.

I felt safe at church. It was a warm and comfortable place. I was special. *We* were special. Latter-day Saints were the chosen people held in heaven to be born in these last days so we could prepare the earth for the return of Christ. After Jesus's death and resurrection there had been a great apostasy and many truths had been taken from the earth, leaving people in darkness and without prophets. And then the heavens opened once more in 1820 when a fourteen year-old farm boy in New York, Joseph Smith, went into a grove of trees to pray and ask God which church to join. He had a vision of the Father and the Son, who told him that none of the churches were right but that he, Joseph, was called to a great work and would restore the truth that had been lost.

It was wonderful to have the truth and to know that everything I was taught by loving teachers was part of that truth. As a child in Sunday School I learned to be a sunbeam for Jesus…to give like the little stream…to follow the prophet…that I am a child of God… that Jesus once was a little child, a little child like me…that pioneer children sang as they walked and walked and walked and walked.

I had fifteen pioneer ancestors who had walked and walked. My own grandmother, Sarah Oakey Sirrine, walked across the plains to Utah at age eight. My great-great-grandfather, Thomas Morris, in the short-lived war with Mexico in 1847, crossed the country in a long infantry march with a group of U.S. soldiers known as the Mormon Battalion. He wrote that "the second shirt has long since been dispensed with to appease the cravings of hunger." Another great-grandfather, George Warren Sirrine, holding a pickax, was lowered over the sides of the ship *Brooklyn* to break off the ice so the voyage could continue around Cape Horn and arrive at what would become San Francisco. He was one of the first vigilantes to bring law and order to that city, and he later became a founder of Mesa, Arizona. I loved the stories of my pioneer ancestors.

And we still walked. My first eight years were spent in Salt Lake City, and every Pioneer Day, July 24th, the day Brigham Young and the first company of pioneers had arrived with wagons and oxen into the Salt Lake Valley, we had the best celebration ever. There was a children's parade, and we dressed up in our long dresses and sunbonnets and decorated our dogs and our tricycles with crepe paper streamers and proudly circled the block a few times. And there was the big parade down Main Street, one of the biggest in the country, featuring high-stepping horses with tails braided with ribbons...marching bands with tall feathers in their hats...bare-legged, beautiful, baton-twirling girls...and the clowns!...floats featuring the dinosaurs and the seven dwarfs and the smiling, waving "Days of '47" royalty...handcarts and wagons with real oxen...Indians with headdresses and drums. But the most important thing in the parade—and everybody knew this—was an open convertible carrying the prophet and his wife. Nobody in the parade, nobody in the whole United States of America or even the wide world was as important as this man.

For most of my growing up years, the prophet and president of the church was David O. McKay. We loved and revered him. He was tall and handsome, with a full white head of hair, dignified and gentle and smiling. It was easy to believe that he was unusually close to Heavenly Father. I heard once that some people complained to President McKay about the bathing beauties on the parade floats. He smiled and said, "I saw nothing that was not beautiful." He was very accepting like that, never trying to make you be afraid so you'd be good.

As AN ADOLESCENT it was wonderful to know that if we obeyed the rules—didn't smoke or drink alcohol or coffee, paid a tithing to the church, were honest and good and stayed virtuous before marriage, we could be worthy to go to the temple and receive more light and knowledge and be married for time and all eternity to the person we loved. My parents had married that way in the temple—they were "sealed," and that was an especially good thing now because a year before when I was fifteen my mother died after many long and painful months of cancer. Through the awful sadness, I knew that our family was forever. As I had stood by my thin mother's casket at the mortuary during the viewing, I nodded in response to all the people who said to me, "Isn't it wonderful to know that you will see your mother again, that your family will all be together in the celestial kingdom? What a saint your mother was."

Yes, I was sure my mother would qualify for the celestial kingdom.

Our church taught that almost everyone would be assigned to one of three kingdoms of glory in heaven. The only people who will be forever burning and weeping and wailing will be the very few people who are "sons of perdition" and are cast into "outer darkness." Hitler and Judas were the only ones we thought for sure. The lowest of the kingdoms of glory was the "telestial," with a glory like unto the stars. Above that was the "terrestrial kingdom," with a glory like unto the moon.

The only one you really wanted to aim for was the top one, the "celestial kingdom." The glory of this one was like unto the sun and was where Heavenly Father lived. Even in this kingdom there were three levels, and the top one of those was also the only one you wanted to aim for. That top level was for the very, very righteous, and particularly those who had been baptized by proper priesthood authority and had kept the commandments and had been married in the temple and had the ordinance of sealing placed upon them. They would be able to be together with their families forever. The other two levels of the celestial kingdom were for those who had been baptized and kept the commandments but had not been married and sealed in the temple. They would be assigned to be "ministering angels." As I had watched the lid of the casket close, I was certain my mother would qualify for the very, very top layer. And I had to be righteous so that sometime I would be there too.

I remembered something my mother had said a few years before her death, when we were living way out in the land of nowhere on the Ute Indian reservation in eastern Utah in a little town called Gusher on a tiny farm that didn't have electricity or indoor plumbing. Finally we got a kind of gas-operated wringer washing machine that made things a lot easier for my mother. When it worked right. Once, when it didn't, I was shocked to see my mother kick the offending machine and say through tears, "This damn washing machine is keeping me out of the celestial kingdom!"

I don't think I had ever heard my mother swear before, but I didn't think Heavenly Father would be that strict. My mother had been on two separate missions for the church, converting people to the gospel. And, of course, she and my father had been sealed in the temple and so we five children had all been "born in the covenant" and belonged to them forever. I was quite sure she had all the bases covered and would be in the celestial kingdom waiting for us.

My mother had never told me about polygamy in heaven, that it was God's special kind of marriage, and that if we were righteous enough that's how we would be living. Walking home now from school after hearing about it for the first time, I wished she had. She had explained to me why my body would bleed once a month for a few days, and I had found that pretty shocking, but it was nothing compared to what I had just learned. This polygamy thing—it wouldn't happen just once a month, it would happen forever and ever. And if it felt like what I was feeling now, I was guessing it would hurt forever too.

I PUT THAT day away and took out the next one. I used my days well. I was a top student, always got "superiors" or "excellents" at speech competitions, was president of the Thespian club and editor of the school paper. A boy in my class burned a cross on my lawn in the middle of the night because he was jealous of me for being the editor. Daddy was pretty upset at that, and the boy had to pay to have the lawn fixed. I made sure he was noted in the school paper as the "student most likely to reseed." I was clever like that, not one of the popular kids but one of the very smart ones. I won an oration competition and got to represent the state of Utah at the Alexander Hamilton Bicentennial Constitutional Convention in Washington D.C., getting my picture taken with President Eisenhower in the rose garden. At BYU, I got straight As and was a star student in the theatre department and continued to keep myself morally clean. As far as I could tell, I was doing everything right and was creating a very good shot at the celestial kingdom and making Heavenly Father proud of me.

I THOUGHT ABOUT Heavenly Father a lot. I tried not to let him know how disappointed I was in the plan he had for us, at least in the plan he had for women. The specter of eternal polygamy had taken center place in a gallery of many dark thoughts that all testified to a large and burning question. *Why is maleness superior to femaleness?*

I know there are some women who would say that thought has never occurred to them, but to me the fact that maleness is superior to femaleness was not in question. The evidence was all around me. God was male. The voices of authority everywhere were male. In church we prayed to, sang about, studied about males. Nobody in the Bible prayed for a girl child. Obviously there was something about maleness that made it more valuable than femaleness, like gold was more valuable than silver. But *why?* I was female. I was smart. I was good. But God had created girls to be eternally less than boys, who were male just like God was male. I studied about it—everything that could be found, in scripture, in books by the church leaders—I asked people who should know—I prayed about it—I wept about it.

When I was a freshman at BYU, Dr. Bruce B. Clark, my English professor, assigned us to write our weekly theme on "A Fate Worse than Death." I wrote on polygamy, a fate that transcended even death. Dr. Clark gave me an A on the paper with a request that I see him in his office. "I can tell that you are a very thoughtful and passionate young woman, Miss Wright, and a fine writer," he said, "and I'd like to try to help you understand this principle of plural marriage." He posited the situation of a man who had a first and then a second wife and loved them both. Ought he not to be able to be with both of them in the next life?

I listened laboriously. "But…but what about a woman who loved a first and a second husband? Why can't she be with both husbands in the next life?"

He smiled kindly and shook his head. "Well, this is just the way it is. And someday we will understand it."

The polygamy problem sort of faded into the background like the pain of my mother's death or like stories about the Holocaust, and I just moved on with life. After graduating with an M.A. in theatre, teaching at Snow College for a year, and traveling the world for a year, I came back to Provo and fell in love with an irresistible, charming blond young man I met as we were in a play together at BYU, *The Skin of Our Teeth*, by Thornton Wilder. In 1966, Gerald Pearson and I were married in the Salt Lake Mormon temple in a lovely ceremony, sealed for time and all eternity. I did notice that the words uniting us forever were different for him than they were for me. I "gave" myself and "received" him. He "received" me but did not "give" himself. There was no equal giving and receiving. Later it became obvious to me that this difference left the door open to possible plural marriage as a man can "receive" numerous women but a woman can "give" herself only to one man. But I was in love and I was happy and I knew that Heavenly Father was pleased.

In the first year of our marriage we enjoyed going to visit Christy, a poet of local renown quite a bit older than we were. Christy was very faithful in the church, but her husband was what we called "fallen away." One Sunday as Gerald drove us home in the blue Volkswagen we had bought with the money I earned as a writer for BYU's motion picture studio—and this memory, too, is vividly clear in my mind—my husband said nonchalantly, "I think Christy should be one of the wives that I take in the celestial kingdom."

I turned to look at him in horror. "Gerald! Are you *serious?*"

"Well, of course," he said, surprised at my reaction. "That's what it's about—letting every righteous woman be sealed to a righteous priesthood holder. That's why polygamy is part of the gospel plan." Again, that cold tightening in my chest. A divide between me and someone I loved. And a further divide between me and God.

That Gerald had no interest in collecting women is well known. He was gay. He had told me of his past feelings and experiences during our engagement, but we both believed what our church taught, that this was just a mistake, a sin from which you repent. We married, confident that all would be well. Eventually I wrote a book about our lives together, *Goodbye, I Love You*. In those early years, Gerald was a true believer in Mormonism, deeply orthodox. He had served as a missionary for the church in Australia, and he knew the doctrine: polygamy, which is a divine principle, had to be temporarily abandoned on this earth, but would probably be restored before the millennium and would absolutely meet us again in heaven if we're righteous enough, which he and I certainly would be.

LONG STORY VERY short. That good, smart girl—that questioning young woman—found answers. I have maintained activity in our church, in this Mormon community that I so love. But I now know for myself that the idea that maleness is more important than femaleness is a sad relic passed from generation to generation throughout most of history, a relic that not only is false but profoundly harmful to all humans of both genders. And I am personally persuaded that the Ghost of Eternal Polygamy exists today from error, that plural marriage never was—is not now—and never will be ordained of God.

I had no intention of ever addressing this subject in a public way. But then something startled me into realizing that those terrible teachings about polygamy that I had personally thrown away are still alive and vicious and harming people I care about. Not long ago I was in Utah visiting with a cousin then in her mid-nineties, "Charlotte," whom I had loved and admired all my life. Her husband "George" had passed away ten years before. As Charlotte and I were enjoying our usual ritual—chatting and reminiscing while she reclined on the couch and I gave her a long foot massage with lotion—I said, "So, Charlotte, you and I are both getting on in years. One of these days we're going to cross over to the other side. How do you feel about that?"

"Oh," she said, "I feel just fine about that." But then a cloud crossed her face. "Only—only I wonder—I wonder if George has taken another wife already."

A little shock ran through me. *Another wife already!* How many times had I sat in that room and heard her husband tell me how lucky he was to be the one that Charlotte chose. I had sometimes seen tears in his eyes when I heard him speak of how much he loved her. This was the man who, since their honeymoon, placed a glass of ice water on the small table on her side of the bed because she got thirsty in the night and he did not. Even after his stroke the ritual continued, and the ice in the glass tinkled as he shuffled along with his little gift of love.

I stopped massaging my cousin's feet and stared at her. "No, Charlotte. No! George has not taken another wife! Of course not!"

"Well," she said with a shrug and a sigh of resignation. "That's what we're taught."

As I LEFT her home that day my sadness turned to anger. My cousin should have been able to spend her last days in peaceful anticipation of greeting again the husband who had so adored her. But instead, she was entertaining the thought—planted by her religion—that he had already begun to create his celestial circle of wives. To me this was extraordinary spiritual abuse.

I knew she was not alone in this fear. I knew there were many women, in the valleys of Utah and across all of Mormondom, who experienced a similar haunting. For decades, since the publication of my first book, I had received and kept many letters from LDS women who found in me a sister they could confide in. Among those letters was one from a woman in North Carolina: "I have spent many nights in tears since my temple marriage a little over a year ago. I feel so much love for my husband that the knowledge that I may have to share him with others has become 'a fire in my mind' and has shaken me to the core. How do I work toward a celestial glory that I dread with all my heart? I turn to you now humbly seeking your help."

I had no help to give this sister in 1976, only to tell her that I mourned with her. But I was stronger now. The Ghost, I knew, was a formidable figure, well established and well protected. But I had faced him down in my own life, had evicted him from my personal house of faith. What if I—what if many of us together—could summon the fortitude and determination of our pioneer ancestors who walked across the plains and gave birth under wagons in the rain and helped to carve out great beauty in the wilderness? I began to believe we could accomplish a new victory for a new day—that we could find the power to cast the Ghost from our community once and for all.

Other Voices:

A celestial glory that I dread with all my heart

THE WOMEN AND men who sent me their stories through the survey I sponsored, as well as a few that brought them to me in other ways, echo the poignant words in that letter from 1976. These are not exactly "voices from the dust." Instead, they are perhaps "voices from the shadow," coming from a side of our Mormon culture on which light has yet to fall. From the thousands of painful stories that have come to me, I could choose only a fraction to include in this book. It is a great privilege for me to pass the talking stick to members of our tribe who have never before been heard. Your privilege, in this and the "Other Voices" sections that follow most of the subsequent chapters, is to listen.

Recently my highly orthodox mother and I had a conversation that I found devastating. She said, "The one thing that would cause me to lose my faith and leave the church would be if a bishop called your dad and me in and told us that we had been chosen to practice polygamy. I couldn't do it. I will never do it."

I said, "Even if you truly thought the instruction came straight from God?"

"Even then. I don't care who it came from."

This shocked me because my mother had never given even a whisper of disagreeing with God or his church about anything! I asked her, "Mom, what will you do in the afterlife, in the celestial kingdom? What will you do when Dad has been given plural wives to populate his 'worlds without number'?"

She replied with a sad smile, "Oh, sweetie, I won't be there."

Confused, I asked, "You won't be in the celestial kingdom? You're the best woman I know! How can you say you won't be there?"

"Well, I make sure that I commit little sins—nothing big—just little sins like lying and being judgmental and other things—just enough so I don't have to go to the highest level of the celestial kingdom. So I'll never have to worry about that polygamy stuff."

"Does Dad know this?"

"Yes. We've talked about it and he understands."

"So—so you won't be with Dad in heaven?"

Sadly, Mom shook her head and said, "I just try not to think of it too much."

Two weeks after my mother passed in October, Dad was dating and by June he was engaged. My brothers and I were crushed to find out, on the day of the wedding, that they were actually being sealed in the temple. It felt like Mom died all over again. She had no say in this—and now she would be a plural wife forever and ever! My grim hope is that when both Dad and Stepmom step through the veil, Mom's there with her own fiery sword. I have not been back to the temple since their sealing. One of my brothers didn't get out of bed for two days after the wedding.

When I finally made the very difficult decision, with the blessing of my adult children, to cancel the sealing to my late first husband so I could be sealed to my second husband, whom I also dearly love—I had to pay a very, very high price.

It has cost me a forty-year happy relationship with my first husband's family. They literally disowned me. If we have a family baptism or baby blessing they will come to the church but they won't come to the lunch/dinner after if I will be there. They took my name off of all of the family lists. Many of them do not even speak to me anymore.

It should not have to be this way! My deepest wish is that these policies might change, that someday other women will not have to bear the burden of choosing between two righteous men, one who has passed on and one who shares the journey here. Men do not have to choose. Only women do. I do not believe God works this way.

My father is currently sealed to three living women. He is divorced from the first two and married to the third. He freely claims them all as wives sealed to him, and also claims the children from my mother's non-temple remarriage. He seems very pleased about this.

As for me, I am the gay spouse in a mixed-orientation temple marriage. I feel like I have been tyrannized my whole life by Mormon conceptions of marriage. They don't fit me either as a woman or as a homosexual.

My husband's first wife had an affair that resulted in a baby. Also in a divorce. Not long after, she had another affair with a different man and had another baby. My husband has tried without success to have the sealing to his first wife cancelled. So that means, if you believe LDS doctrine, that in the eternities my husband and I and our children *and the first wife and her two children* (who were born in the covenant of the first marriage) will make up a "forever family." Who can believe this notion came from God?

I believe that eternal polygamy is the secret sacred cow of the patriarchy, the collective expectation of eternal harems held by many Mormon men. I've seen countless marriages damaged by belief in eternal polygamy. If a man's marriage is not what he may want in some area, or if he just has a wandering eye—great!—he has options in the next world. I have seen more than one married Mormon man lining up women for a marriage in the next life. I also believe that it contributes to the well-known LDS porn epidemic, by encouraging "window shopping." And even worse, if a man's mind is already sort of crazy, the idea of polygamy can lead to a fourteen-year-old girl being taken from her bed at knife point.

My daughter was raised in the church and had a very strong testimony of it. She began dating a non-member boy who quickly took the missionary discussions and joined the church, which confirmed in her mind that he was the right one for her. They were married for eternity in the temple and soon had a baby. Life seemed good.

Her new husband had attended weekly priesthood meeting for barely six months when he became fixated on the topic of polygamy. This all came out one day when she said to me, "Mom, I've been realizing that the church actually believes I was created to be part of a giant baby-making plan designed to make men have this special glory with all their wives. And I don't have the good feeling I've always had about the gospel." I was shocked. I listened to this wonderful, smart, beautiful daughter of mine explain how she felt like a nobody.

Soon, my daughter's young and restless new husband was talking about polygamy to everyone, even behaving as if he were in a special fraternity at church with other young husbands, all of which only served to make my daughter feel more estranged.

Was this church of ours truly "especially for men"? How had these teachings so quickly affected the man she loved? And how had this influenced the divorce that soon followed as he grew more and more distant and then adopted behavior that eventually led to cheating?

How many other Mormon men damage their marriages with this strange escape of thinking about the future wives they will get to enjoy in the celestial kingdom?

As I spend time helping my daughter recover from that disaster of a marriage, she's earned several medical degrees and licenses, and is rebuilding her self-esteem. But somehow, deep down, she and I both still know that she is not held in high esteem by the Mormon Church. And that is not okay with me.

As I grew older and remained single, I began to hear many more comments directed to me about not "losing faith" because I would be sealed to a righteous man as one of his many wives in the next life. I remember one day in church looking around the congregation at couples and families and realizing, in order for me to marry, I have to either wait for one of these women to die, or for me to die. It was a depressing thought, and one that was a large factor in me beginning to date outside the church when I was in my late twenties and eventually leave the fold.

Polygamy became very real for me when my parents divorced after thirty years. My father took solace in his belief that in heaven he will not only enjoy the eternal company of his new wife, but also have my mother. These two wonderful women are aware of his feelings and aware that the church, which they hold dear, teaches this. It causes them both pain and has caused my father and his new wife to move far away so she would not have to run into her "sister wife" at the grocery store or the post office.

My parents were sealed in the SLC temple, and when I was thirteen years old my father was killed in an accident. My mother remarried when I was sixteen, and she and her second husband were together for thirty-four years before he passed away a few years ago. Prior to his passing, my mother had her sealing to my father cancelled and was sealed to her second husband. This did not set well with me. My vision of our eternal family was shattered and the whole thing caused much friction in our family. Many feelings were hurt. Many unkind words were said. It was a mess at best.

And what about my father?—the odd man out who had no voice in this? I was very upset with my mother and deeply upset with the church for allowing this. I think it is very presumptuous for church authorities to think they know how the next life is going to look as far as who is married to whom and meddle around the way they do. I think they have made a giant mess of the whole thing. And I don't believe that polygamy was ever commanded by God.

Perhaps if the church did not have such a limited position on families, perhaps I might have been able to feel of some eternal worth growing up. Perhaps today I would not have such deep resentment to overcome and such a lot to forgive—feeling rejected for not fitting in, for not being in a "sealed" family, feeling looked down on by various bishops I have had to interact with.

I don't believe Jesus ever intended for the souls of man, the hearts of children, to be wounded through his church. In fact, I believe it saddens him when his children are made to feel less worthy or less important to him because they are a woman or are a child in a dysfunctional family.

Could someone please explain to me the logic in this? A person can be excommunicated from the church by the authority of any bishop or stake president, and it can be done in a matter of days, this thing that is supposedly the worst thing that can ever happen to a person as it cancels his or her "claim upon eternal life." *But* it requires the authority held by only three men, the First Presidency, and takes months if not years and often never, to have a marriage sealing broken, even if both parties hope never to see each other again.

I divorced my first husband, to whom I had been "sealed" in the temple, because he was emotionally abusive and cruel to me about sex for years. Only after we were divorced did he admit to having an addiction to pornography. Being still sealed to him was worrisome to me because he would tell me that I had gotten rid of him now, but that we're still married in God's eyes.

My being previously sealed did turn off a couple of potential suitors, who wanted a wife who could be theirs for eternity. I felt pretty worthless, as if I were damaged goods, even among the Saints. I had a couple of friends actually tell me that if I didn't marry again in this life, they'd allow their husbands to take me as another wife in heaven. For as generous a gesture as it was, it made me feel hopeless and like I'd only ever be someone's "extra wife," never truly loved. You can't imagine how awful eternity and the highest kingdom looks from that vantage point.

Eventually I found a man who truly loved me. What I appreciated most was how he was not bound to the LDS ideal or promise of polygamy, as he was a long-time inactive member. He didn't want more wives; I was and am enough for him. I feel like a goddess with him in a way I never did when pressed and manipulated by men's ideas of the "sacred rite" of eternal marriage and polygamy. I no longer think about having to share my husband or worry about how polygamy will work because I believe it is a total falsehood. I don't live in fear of that anymore. No woman should have to.

My first husband, to whom I was sealed, left me because he did not want to be a father. A few years later, I married one of the best men on the planet, one who doesn't care much for the temple. And now we have a house full of beautiful children who love their father wholly and completely, and their father loves them. Fatherhood comes naturally to him—more naturally than motherhood comes to me. And yet, these beautiful children are not sealed to him. They are sealed to a stranger they've never met, a stranger who took active steps to prevent himself from being a parent now or in the eternities.

And how do we explain this to our children when it comes up in Primary? How about—your parents aren't sealed, but you are part of an eternal family unit that doesn't include this father that you adore? Not going to do that. We're not singing about how families can be together forever. We're just living that right here and now. And when we all do get to heaven, surely we will be together in whatever way "together" looks over there. And it won't be because of anything this church institution has done. It's going to be only because of the graciousness, mercy, love and compassion of Heavenly Parents who don't care about bureaucracy and nineteenth-century definitions of success, patriarchal prosperity, and eternal kingship.

[Joseph] Smith was an authentic religious genius, unique in our national history.... I do not find it possible to doubt that [he] was an authentic prophet. Where in all of American history can we find his match?... In proportion to his importance and his complexity, [Joseph Smith] remains the least-studied personage, of an undiminished vitality, in our entire national saga.

—Harold Bloom, literary critic

-2-
Brother Joseph

I'VE NEVER SEEN a vision, but I've always wanted to. The closest I've ever come is when I played Joan of Arc on the BYU stage in Anouilh's *The Lark*. Night after night of performance and through all the wonderful rehearsals, I got to see Joan's visions, those shining angels, St. Michael and St. Margaret and St. Catherine. I created them in my mind's eye the best I knew how, and they were very beautiful, so I kind of knew how it felt to have a vision. Joan gave me a number of gifts that have stayed with me through the years. I learned how it felt to say yes to a really hard task, how it felt to say no to authority, and how it felt to be true to your beliefs no matter the price. I kept my black corduroy Joan of Arc boots with their soft felt soles and laces that came up to the knee, even though I should have turned them in to the costume department after the final performance when we "struck the set." I believe our director, Dr. Hansen, would not have minded my keeping them. Once in a while over the years when I needed some extra courage, I've taken Joan's boots out of my "archive" box, laced them up and worn them for a day. It's good to feel Joan's bravery traveling up my body.

I KNOW THERE are visionaries. I know there are seers. I believe that Joseph Smith was one of them. Often we sing at church:

> Praise to the man who communed with Jehovah!
> Jesus anointed him Prophet and Seer.
> Blessed to open the last dispensation,
> Kings shall extol him and nations revere.

As a Mormon girl I had learned about the remarkable visions of Joseph Smith. The fuller story, knowing that Joseph was not unique on the path of the visionary, makes me appreciate God more and doesn't make me appreciate Joseph less. A contemporary of Joseph, Ellen White, reported more than a hundred visions and helped to found the Seventh-day Adventist Church. A few decades before Joseph was born, William Blake, the English poet, claimed to have had his first vision at age ten, a tree full of angels. A century prior to Joseph, Swedish scientist and mystic Emanuel Swedenborg told of the heavens opening to him in dreams and visions, showing him the true nature of the soul. And back in the middle ages, mystics galore were having experiences with heaven. Dame Julian of Norwich received fifteen consecutive visions and revelations in one night and another the following day, experiences that filled her with godly insights.

Joseph's visionary experiences with the Father and the Son, with angels and many other heavenly personages, brought something unique. They produced an inspired text, the Book of Mormon, more than 500 pages long, dictated in ninety days and listed in 2013 by the Library of Congress as one of the one hundred most influential "Books that Made America." But beyond that, Joseph's interactions with the divine led him to wed heaven and earth in such a way that a vibrant new society was born, more than a clan or a tribe or a church, an actual spiritual family of brothers and sisters called to be a covenant and godly people. I feel honored to have been born into this group.

I CAN'T BE counted as a scholar on the life of the Prophet Joseph Smith, but I lived quite intimately with him for more than two years. In 1977, I got a call from Jim Conkling, a music and broadcasting executive in Hollywood who helped create the Grammy Awards and the Columbia Record Club.

"Carol Lynn," he said after he introduced himself, "I've been put in charge of what I think is a very important project. The brethren in Salt Lake want to see a motion picture produced on the life of the Prophet Joseph. This hasn't been done before. They've got the money for it, but want it to be a non-church project. It has to show Joseph in a good light, of course, but also be honest. We're inviting six writers to each create a screenplay, and if all goes well we'll choose the best one for full production. Are you interested?"

"Well...I'm...honored. Um...'honest,' you said. Does this mean you're going to get into...polygamy?"

"Yep. Have to. It won't be the main thing, but it'll be there. Think it over."

I was flooded with a wave of anxiety. When I hung up the phone, I grabbed my hat and sunglasses and went for a hike to the top of the nearby hills, a reflex when I needed to think something through. Why was I hesitating? This was a real movie, not just an educational film like the ones I had written for BYU's motion picture studio a few years earlier. Why was my excitement overcast with unease?

I climbed and thought...*Joseph Smith*...*Joseph Smith*...*Joseph Smith*—that familiar, foreign, revered, frightening territory, *Joseph Smith*. For a long time I had kept the Prophet Joseph at arm's length—he was the one who had established polygamy as the order of God's highest heaven—and I had a complicated relationship, too, with the church that he organized. I had always been an "active" Mormon and had received a lot of good things from being a member of the church. But pain was there as well. It was sort of like embracing a very good man who steps on your toes. The pain was a two-pronged grief—"women's issues" and "gay issues."

The "gay issues" pain had been building for three years, ever since it was clear that my husband Gerald was not "cured" of his homosexuality. Those three years had been excruciating for both of us. Being with a woman who truly loved him had not worked. Repentance and prayer and fasting had not worked. Nothing our church had offered had worked.

Gerald and I and our four children had just moved from Provo, Utah, to Walnut Creek, California. If it came to a divorce, I didn't want to play that out in Utah, not in front of so many people who by now knew my name. The first year of our marriage, Gerald had insisted on publishing a little book of my poems, *Beginnings*, which by fluke or by fate put me on the map in Mormondom. I didn't want so many people who had come to love my work seeing me through embarrassment and pity, and seeing Gerald through condemnation. Like most people, Mormons had a knowledge of homosexuality that was pretty much still in the dark ages. A church should be a refuge in times of grief. But what if the refuge had helped cause the grief? "Blossom," I remember Gerald saying one day, "the biggest problem is this. I love the church, but the church detests me." He and so many others had been told by the highest authorities in the church that they would be better off dead than to live life as an active homosexual. I felt that our church had failed us both on this issue. Still, that wasn't Joseph's fault.

But "women's issues," with the whole mess of polygamy dead center—that *was* Joseph's fault. Unless it was *God's* fault. I still sometimes entertained that terrible thought.

Looking down at my neighborhood from the top of the grassy green hills was always useful. A widened view. I should do it. Maybe if I immersed myself totally in Joseph's life I could come to understand some things, solve some puzzles once and for all. And so I began my two-year residency with the Prophet Joseph Smith.

JIM SENT EACH writer boxes and boxes of material—books, copies of unavailable books, scholarly periodicals, monographs, timelines, stories from those who had known Joseph, papers of all kinds. I asked Jim to find certain documents for me, and he found them. I read, made notes, did interviews, wrote, rewrote. If I wasn't studying or writing about Joseph, I was thinking about him. He and I became very close during that time. I had always admired Joseph, but I was surprised at how easy it was to sincerely like him.

The fact is this ambitious motion picture project was never completed. After two years of writing and rewriting, meetings and readings, I learned that the project was put on hold. The powers at church headquarters could not agree on how to represent their founding prophet, and so no film was made. Mine was one of two scripts that had made it through to the end, and I received a lot of good comments about it. The main criticisms mine received were that it was "too sympathetic to Joseph's wife Emma, and also too sympathetic to Joseph's friends who turned against him at the end." As of this writing, a major motion picture about Joseph Smith has yet to be made.

Not long ago I located my screenplay and read through it. "Brother Joseph—the American Prophet" was my title. This was not a great screenplay. It was too theatrical, depended too much on dialogue. But I did a pretty good job, I think, of telling the story and drawing the character of Joseph. Much of his story is heavy and hard to tell—he and his people faced brutality, hardships, disease, arrests, an extermination order, and finally Joseph's assassination. But always there is that marvelous optimism, that maddening self-confidence, Joseph's belief that he could not fail. I had come to Joseph thinking I would keep him at arm's length, but time after time I found my arms around him. I liked him, and—dare I say it—I even loved him.

I OPENED THE screenplay on the road coming into the frontier town of Far West, Missouri, in 1838, as two hundred covered wagons complete their arrival. Joseph, six feet tall, light brown hair, piercing blue eyes, athletic, greets people he has never seen before as if they were close friends. "Welcome to Zion! It's good to have you here!" He sweeps six year-old James off the wagon and into his arms. "Especially the little fellers. Children get the front row seats in the kingdom of God. What's your name, son?"

"James," says the boy, timidly.

"James, do you know who I am?"

The boy looks up reverently at Joseph. "Are you the Lord?"

Joseph throws back his head and laughs. "Just his brother. And so are you. We're all of us—all—brothers and sisters."

I wrote a theme song for the film. It came in here as Brother Joseph continues to walk down the train of wagons, greeting the newcomers.

> Brothers and Sisters—hold out your hands.
> Let me touch you—help you understand
> That we are Brothers and Sisters—all family.
> Your joys are my joys—and your hurts hurt me.
>
> Way down within us—where spirit is flowing—
> There moves the dream—the vision, the knowing
> That from the beginning God's breath was inside us.
> There is no ending—not death can divide us.
>
> Brothers and Sisters—hold out your hands.
> Love one another 'til everyone stands
> As Brothers and Sisters—sharing the sun—
> Learning at last—that we are one.

Joseph gives a short, fiery address, welcoming the new Saints to "our poverty and our love." Then he says, "Now, anybody who has not had supper—which includes me—and anybody who has something left over, meet right up here for an introduction."

WE'RE GOING TO move from simple to complex as I introduce you to the Joseph that I came to love. There is endless information about and interpretations of this man and his work. I will just share some snapshots that I took as I walked along the paths of his personality, his character, noting small actions that loom large. Many of these I wove into the screenplay. To me they were not frivolous. These little moments help to answer the questions—Why did this man draw so many to him?—Why was he so loved?—Why was he so resented? As we move toward the end of this inadequate sketch, we will move out of the sunlight and into the shadow. See the following as possible scenes on screen, each based in fact.

EMMA, JOSEPH'S WIFE, is asleep as he tiptoes into the bedroom. Without even opening her eyes, she says, "I see you've given away another pair of boots. Any other woman who catches her husband coming in stocking-footed knows he's spent the night at the grog shop. When mine comes in like that, I know he's given away another pair of boots."

Joseph replies, "I'll get another pair somewhere." Emma pulls him down and kisses him warmly.

JOSEPH ACCOMPANIES HIS friends to the polls to vote at Gallatin. A group of Missourians insist they will not be allowed to vote, they're not real Americans, they're Mormons, and Joseph is a fraud, stealing sheep from the true fold of Christ.

Joseph asks, "Will you believe I'm a prophet if I whip you to prove it?"

A big man, George, steps up and says, "You whip me, and I'll believe you're a prophet!"

"How much do you weigh, Mister?" asks Joseph.

"When I'm good natured I weight a hundred and ninety pounds. When I'm mad I weigh a ton."

The Missourians laugh. Joseph takes off his coat. Joseph and George circle each other for a moment, then George lunges at Joseph. Joseph whirls around, catches him deftly by the collar and the belt and rushes him headlong into a large ditch a few feet away. Missourians and Mormons laugh.

Joseph says, "I just can't help baptizing a sinner when I see one."

IN THE MIDST of a very tense meeting with the brethren, Joseph calls them all outside and leads them in a snowball fight. John Taylor, always serious, balks.

Joseph says, "Oh, come on, John! I can't have an apostle who won't laugh!"

"Now?" John replies, "Now, while the mobbers rage?"

"Especially now while the mobbers rage!" says Joseph as he aims a snowball at his friend and follower. "And after we've got our spirits up, we'll get back to business."

JOSEPH'S GENEROSITY AND compassion are large to a fault. Though the prophet, he is expected to earn a living. In Nauvoo, the city they built on a swamp, the Red Brick Store is constructed specifically for him so he can serve as shopkeeper, selling dry goods and groceries. But within a few months the store goes bankrupt. Joseph cannot turn away anyone who needs anything, whether they have money or not.

AT A TIME when many religions forbid dancing and music, Joseph starts a theatre in Nauvoo. He encourages dancing. He loves being with his people, socializing. Emma says, "Joseph can never eat by himself. He must have his friends with him."

JOSEPH OFFENDS SOME of the brethren by doing "women's work" like carrying out the ashes and carrying in the water, and by ice skating with his children.

To a young black woman, Jane James, who joined the church, traveled to Nauvoo, and finds herself without a place to stay, Joseph says:

"Emma, here's a girl who says she's got no home. Don't you think she's got a home here?"

Emma replies, "Of course, if she wants to stay."

"Here?" asks Jane, amazed. "You mean I could stay with you—just like I was your very own servant?"

"Well, no," says Joseph. Disappointed, Jane looks down. "But," Joseph goes on, "you could stay—and help out just like you were family."

Jane shrieks, then throws her arms around both Joseph and Emma.

JOSEPH PREACHES TO a small group of onlookers as he and two sheriffs water their horses at a stream. He is under arrest on old charges of treason and is being taken back to Missouri. But, in the best of the wild-west tradition, they look up and see 175 men of Joseph's "Nauvoo Legion" thundering toward them. Joseph speaks to the dumbfounded sheriffs, "Well, I guess I won't go to Missouri today. Those are my boys!"

A SHORT WHILE later at the "Mansion House" in Nauvoo, the two sheriffs, Wilson and Reynolds, sit uncomfortably at the head of a large table. About fifty people are present. Joseph comes by with a tray laden with food. "More pie, Mr. Reynolds?" Reynolds is loath to take Joseph Smith's food, but he is hungry and holds out his plate.

NAUVOO IS PLAGUED with malaria and large numbers are sick and dying. Joseph and Emma pitch a tent and sleep outside their house so some of the sick can have beds.

DURING A FRIGHTENING incident in which the carriage he is riding in finds itself with runaway horses and no driver, Joseph calms a terrified woman who is fearful the coach will roll over and is about to throw her baby out the window to save its life. He then climbs along the outside to the driver's seat and finally brings the horses to a halt. At the end of the journey the relieved passengers find that the man they were thanking for his courage is the Mormon Prophet.

ANTHONY, A FREE black man, is arrested and fined for selling liquor in Nauvoo on the Sabbath and pleads with Joseph, the mayor, for leniency, saying he did it to get money to buy his child, who is still a slave in a Southern state. Joseph says justice must be served, but then adds: "See that horse over there? It's a fine horse. It used to belong to me, but now it belongs to you. I want you to sell that horse, pay the fine, and use the rest of the money to buy the freedom of your child."

ON THE LONG march to reclaim their losses in Missouri known as "Zion's Camp," a very difficult and in many ways a disastrous trek, Joseph refuses any special treatment. He is offered sweet bread, but refuses it, asking for the sour bread the others are eating. Rather than choosing to ride on the supply wagons, Joseph walks with the other men twenty-five to forty miles a day in the heat on blistered and bloody feet.

KNOWING THAT AT any moment his enemies could overtake him, Joseph sleeps with his feet against the door and a loaded musket at his side.

JOSEPH "ELECTRIFIES" HIS audience as he preaches that man is God's work and God's glory, that creeds circumscribe truth and that what he wants is "expansion," embracing good wherever it may be found, proving all things and holding fast that which is righteous, giving his hearers words that make them feel progressive and forward-looking.

And telling his Twelve Apostles, "A man filled with the love of God is not content with blessing his family alone, but ranges through the whole world anxious to bless the whole human family."

THESE ARE THE simple stories that make it very easy to love or at least admire Joseph. But his is not a small story, and so the plot has to thicken. And for the "tragic hero," which it can be argued Brother Joseph surely was, the plot line becomes classically clear. Aristotle in his *Poetics* says a tragic hero is one "whose misfortune is brought about not by vice or depravity, but by some error or frailty."

We Mormons don't like to look at the errors of our prophet-heroes. And we quickly come to the conclusion that it may look like a mistake but it really wasn't, that God was in charge and this thing that looks bad had to happen for the larger good. Either way, the plot thickens. And among all the people we call "prophets," why would Brother Joseph be the only one who did not err large?

We read that Hamlet's tragic flaw was his indecisiveness. He delayed necessary action and thus caused terrible harm. Might Joseph's tragic flaw have been the opposite? Joseph's biographers, those who today are faithful to the church he founded as well as those who have no reason to be partial to Joseph, paint a picture with strokes that suggest a tragic hero who acted sometimes recklessly: he placed quick and unjustified confidence in people who turned out to be traitorous; he was not economically realistic, attempting far more than he or his people could manage, running up debts that plagued him all his life and fleeing from a financial disaster that he himself caused and that nearly destroyed his church; he was overly optimistic, overlooking the practical obstacles in a plan and going ahead anyway, often to fail; he prophesied success for a rash venture, then blamed his followers for their lack of worthiness when it failed; he could be obstinate when contradicted; he believed all of his revelations, never questioning, never doubting that they came from God, and making proclamations—in the words of Mormon scholar Eugene England—"in the full flush of classic hubris." Mormon historian B.H. Roberts put it this way: "The Prophet lived his life in crescendo." That sounds like the kind of character the Furies will surely take down.

If Hamlet demurred when it was time to act, the Prophet Joseph dared and dared large. I remember now their two most famous speeches. Hamlet speaks quietly to himself, "To be, or not to be: that is the question." He yearns for the end that death brings but is afraid that a dream might survive. Joseph, on the other hand, shouts into the wind to a crowd of several thousand followers on a day close to his death the assurance that there can never be an end because there never was a beginning, that the soul of man is co-eternal with God. "Nothing can be destroyed! Intelligence is eternal!"

No wonder Hamlet waits. No wonder Joseph strikes. It's Joseph's huge voraciousness that interests me, for it led to his downfall, his death by murder. Prophet-watchers in surrounding towns, even in his own, looked on uneasily. They watched his hunger build—multiplicity of wives—man to become like God—uniformed lieutenant general of an army two-thirds the size of the national militia—candidate for president of the United States—where will it end?

No question that Joseph used his people, asking of them more and more. He used his people as building blocks, but the edifice they were creating was for each of them just as much as it was for him. Joseph was surprisingly democratic in offering heaven to everyone (and he said he would die to defend the rights of a Baptist as quickly as those of a Mormon). These building blocks were not for a new Tower of Babel that would raise people up closer to God, but were building blocks for a temple that would bring God down to his people. Heaven was to be an immediate experience. In the temple they would bathe in holiness, dress in holiness, be endowed with a holiness they could carry with them as they walked the fallen earth, lifting them higher than before. It was too much holiness for Mr.

Sharp, who published the neighboring *Warsaw Signal*, and for others who also despised the upstart Mormons.

SOMEDAY THERE WILL be a movie made of Joseph's life; it is a historical inevitability. But as I have immersed myself again in the life of the Prophet, I have found that I am caught in a kind of hallowed amazement, and something in me wants to watch the story of Joseph—not in a movie theatre with popcorn and candy—not on the couch where we can stop the streaming to make that call we had forgotten. To me Joseph's story is wide and deep and worthy of utter attention, worthy of a Greek amphitheater, worthy of the year 400 B.C., worthy of the pen of Euripides or Sophocles.

I want to sit in the sun in the huge amphitheater around the stone stage with other citizens of Athens and even slaves, required by law to attend, for this is where we learn of morality, justice, ethics, and the gods. The audience knows the story already, knows the horrors about to take place, but still they look at Medea, look at Oedipus, look at Antigone and say, *don't...don't...please don't...*I whisper the words too...*Joseph, don't...please don't....* Now I find myself onstage as part of the Chorus, the all-seeing Greek Chorus that understands higher and wider than others and makes the awfulness have meaning, makes the theme sing so clearly that the audience cannot leave in innocence.

I played the Nurse once in *Medea,* the horrific story of the mad mother who kills her own children to reap revenge on her husband Jason who has spurned her and taken another wife. I open the playbook now to the early pages to find the first words of the Chorus. Joseph, Emma, listen, there is synchronicity here. Medea has just yearned "that lightning from heaven would split my head open... and leave my hateful existence behind me." The Chorus speaks:

O God and Earth and Heaven!
Did you hear what a cry was that
Which the sad wife sings?...

Suppose your man gives honour
To another woman's bed.
It often happens. Don't be hurt.
God will be your friend in this.
You must not waste away
Grieving too much for him who shared your bed.

Betrayal of the marriage bed is often a theme of tragedy. Joseph's extravagant reinvention of marriage was an open secret in Nauvoo and an open scandal in neighboring towns where Victorian morals were deeply held. To those who believed, Joseph's polygamy came from God. To those who did not, it was of the devil. To all, it was gigantic—it was Bible big, too big. It was not Joseph's wife Emma who plotted revenge, but Joseph's enemies, the ones who used to be his friends alongside ones who had always hated him. Joseph's last large act that brought down the wrath of the Furies was—in his position as mayor of Nauvoo and with the support of his city council—ordering the destruction of a new printing press that had published the *Nauvoo Expositor,* a newspaper that had put into words strong accusations against the Prophet, calling him a "base scoundrel," a "blood thirsty and murderous...demon" and, perhaps most troublesome, describing his very real but denied plural marriages as "whoredoms and abominations."

The deed done, the press in pieces on the street, we enter the last act. Things happen quickly...law and order pitted against the passions of the outraged...a call for Joseph's assassination...Nauvoo, an armed camp...Joseph must choose to give himself up for arrest for treason or see his people slaughtered...*if my life is of no value to my friends it is of no value to me*...the long, slow ride to Carthage where Governor Ford has promised protection and due process.

If the story were truly told by the Greeks, a messenger would run onstage to speak the rest of the tale, breathless and with vowels that are the cry of a wounded bird...how Joseph and his brother Hyrum and their friends John and Willard had been placed in the upper room of the jail for protection…a whisper, *are you afraid to die?*…how the governor left the men in the merciless protection of soldiers who hated them… *A poor wayfaring man of grief…sing it again*…gunshots…two hundred armed men with blackened faces rush the jail, up the stairs…more shots…Hyrum down first… Joseph at the window ready to leap…shot from the back, from the front…falling, falling to the ground…Joseph the Prophet…dead.

The Chorus moans and chants the loss.

The audience in the amphitheater sits quiet for minutes, then each gets up and goes to their home.

I HAVE BEEN to Nauvoo several times, and each time as I have traveled the road to Carthage and back I have said to the driver, "Please don't talk, I want to just be with Joseph." It is impossible to travel that road and not watch the scenes unfold—to see the thousands of Saints that line the road to Nauvoo waiting and weeping, then weeping more loudly as they finally see—approaching the City of Joseph—a single wagon carrying two oak boxes covered with brush to protect their contents from the sun.

Those onlookers make up a kind of Greek Chorus of their own, desolate thousands together crying the witness…crying the loss …crying the *how can we bear it?*…crying the love. Whatever you believe about this man, do not think that Joseph did not love his people, never think that. Time after time he told them he would die for them, and they knew and feared that he would. His people had come by the thousands, across ocean and land, had met him, heard him, watched him and loved him. One wrote what many had experienced, that the Prophet "wrapped his arms around me and squeezed me to his bosom and said: 'George A., I love you, as I do my own life.'"

That is the kind of love that makes tragedy, makes thousands of people line the road bewildered that the "*deus ex machina*" had not lowered from the heavens to save their prophet. They are a Chorus of confusion without script, without meaning, asking *why?...what now?...what can we do?...where can we turn?*

I watch and I weep with them, for I still love Brother Joseph.

I love him after the pattern of Emma Hale Smith.

I love him with a heart that he broke a long time ago.

Other Voices:

"Ye have broken the hearts of your tender wives"

It makes me sad to think about an eternity in which I live in complete fidelity with my husband, but he does not live in complete fidelity with me. It is confusing to me to think that that would be a "higher" state of marriage. The issue of eternal polygamy has caused me deep pain since I first came to understand it as a ten year-old. I've spent three decades seeking to reconcile my soul to it, or trying to "put it on the back burner." Inevitably, that pot ends up boiling over and I have to consider, again and again, the implications of what this doctrine represents and what it says about my value in the economy of the Gods.

I wish today's church leaders would take seriously the message about polygamy in Jacob 2:35 of the Book of Mormon: "Ye have broken the hearts of your tender wives...and the sobbings of their hearts ascend up to God against you." Polygamy is still with us. The sobbing of women's hearts is going on all over the church, and our leaders don't seem to care.

When I was younger I believed what the church said about eternal polygamy, and I was terrified to marry, especially to marry an LDS man. When I became engaged at twenty-nine, I had a tearful conversation with my fiancé, pleading with him not to have another woman sealed to him if I died before he did.

I was terrified of having only two options: being trapped in a polygamous eternal marriage against my will, or leaving the celestial kingdom entirely and never seeing my husband or my children in the hereafter. What an awful and ridiculous anxiety to have when you are supposed to be experiencing the joy of getting married!

My mother was petrified of dying because she was the second wife of my father and knew she would have to live polygamy forever. It broke my heart to watch her trying so hard not to die.

My current husband and his first wife were married in the temple and were active Latter-day Saints for years. His wife slept with another man and got pregnant. They divorced before the baby was born. This ex-wife then slept with a different man and got pregnant again. Both of these children are sealed to my husband, even though they are not his children. They were "born in the covenant," with him and that's the way it will stay.

When he and I got married, we talked about getting sealed to each other. As I looked into it, I realized that if I got sealed to my husband, I would be signing on to live in plural marriage in the eternities, since he would then be sealed to two women.

So now, on this earth, I need to make a terrible decision. Do I want to give up my husband in the eternities, or do I want to keep him and live in eternal polygamy? As of today I am not willing to commit to eternal polygamy, so we remain "unsealed." It is very sad for me, because my husband is my other half. He is a wonderful, delightful, kind, loving, and caring man. But according to church doctrine, unless I choose to be sealed into polygamy, he will be with his first wife forever (just like the songs say!) instead of me.

But I'm told that when we're in heaven we will only want to do what God wants us to do, so we will not have jealousy or any of those earthly feelings. So I figure if we are Christlike and exalted and pure, it probably won't matter *who* we are sealed to. When the time comes, I can just be sealed to Joe the Plumber down the street, and my husband can be with his first wife and the two children she had with other men, and we will be all set. For eternity. Sad, but true.

The issue of eternal polygamy has caused me deep spiritual hurt my whole life as an active, returned missionary member of the church. I have struggled so deeply at times with feelings of mistrust for a God who could value me so little as his daughter that he could command such a devastating principle to be followed. I cannot read the words in the Doctrine and Covenants to Emma Smith without feeling the absolute horror of her situation. She seems damned either way.

I have put it on the proverbial shelf many times, but it has a habit of coming crashing down when the weight gets too much to bear. I have wrestled heavily with the possibility of leaving the church, and have currently decided to stay and ignore polygamy because I value the church as a place of goodness and I want to serve there and grow there. But I still haven't been able to really get over my mistrust of God. The pain and guilt arising from doubts have affected my self-worth and future hope in whatever heaven holds. I hope in my soul that women are worth more than that. So I go forward.

Polygamy in heaven has caused me pain that cannot be quantified. It is the only reason that I fear death. It inhibits my ability to trust in a loving and just Heavenly Father. Its effects have been corrosive to my marriage and my soul. My husband loves me deeply, but he does not understand why I feel so much pain over something that may or may not happen. Whether it happens to me or to someone else, it is a principle that is alive and active in the church and causes pain that is very real. I have this vague terror of being erased, like I am just an interchangeable cog, and that terror keeps me awake late at night.

Polygamy has been the source of much of my fear and anguish (oh, and loss of faith). I can remember as a young girl being taught over and over by church leaders and family members how polygamy had its place and was a very good thing to fulfill the purposes of God. I remember feeling guilt and shame for hating the idea of sharing my future husband in heaven. I thought, "I guess I'm not righteous enough or worthy enough to live with God again."

Feelings of shame worsened as I went on a mission and the subject of polygamy plagued me. "You will be expected to practice polygamy if you ever hope to achieve exaltation!" "It's part of the law of consecration." "It will become a modern-day practice in our time." "Bruce R. McConkie said it will absolutely come back when the millennium starts." "What if your sister never married? Wouldn't you want her to be happy and to be exalted? Surely you'd want to share your husband with her."

Several years after my mission I married my husband. Our first year together was filled with anxiety and fear as I thought I was worthless and easily replaceable—not because of my husband's thoughts or actions, but because of what I had been taught. I thought, "He'll just marry some-one better if I die and love her more. I'm just Leah, and in the eternities he'll find his Rachel." I felt terrible.

Long story short. I finally found the courage to just reject the idea of polygamy altogether. I no longer view it as a commandment nor do I view Joseph Smith's practice of it (or any man's practice of it) as sanctioned by God. I live my life and enjoy my marriage without fear—fear of being replaced, fear of having to compete eternally to be the apple of my husband's eye. I am committed to my husband and he's committed to me—just me! And it's wonderful!

I put up with twenty years of infidelity because I thought it would help me prepare to be a sister wife someday in eternity. I finally ended the marriage after I tried to kill myself. I had given up my personal identity to my religion and saw myself as one of potentially many wives. My temple marriage was a painful sham, but I was told by church leaders I needed to stay in it. I am young, barely turned forty. So this was not a genera-tional ideology. This is current brainwashing and it needs to stop.

I remember how my uncle used to joke about polygamy waiting for us in the next life. His jokes always seemed to be at my aunt's expense. He was a wonderful man and loved his wife dearly, so this was not some jerk. But even he would joke about something that I believe pierced his wife's heart. It did mine, and I was just a child. I wonder now why our church leaders don't pay attention to what the Book of Mormon says about polygamy.

At BYU nearly all my roommates and I talked about the possibility of polygamy. For all of us it was something that caused feelings of trepidation or outright hostility.

On the other hand, many of my male friends at BYU were of the opinion that women who didn't fully support the idea of polygamy were just not righteous nor fully living the gospel. When I would try to explain what it feels like for women, many of the guys wouldn't even try to understand.

I have served as bishop and in stake presidencies for twenty years, and I have seen, mostly from women, a lot of angst and sorrow about church teachings such as polygamy. It's understandable, since the policies are vague in many cases, arbitrary, and condescending toward women.

I've heard my true-believing sisters and sister-in-law talking about spiritual polygamy. They joke and say things like, "My number one fear is that if I die, my husband will marry someone prettier than me, and I'll be the ugly wife in heaven." I believe that the LDS Church is inherently sexist and that teachings like polygamy are evil. All of it makes me sad and angry.

I spent many years pushing down the pain and frustration of polygamy so I could be obedient and happy in my church membership. It finally became too huge of an issue, and I had to finally examine the idea once and for all and make a decision. I remember that day. I had spent a lot of time reading about what happened to Emma Smith in regard to Joseph's polygamy. My stomach hurt and I couldn't sleep. I imagined the same thing happening with my own husband and became angry and tearful and even more physically ill.

I then came to realize something remarkable. In my heart I did not believe polygamy came from God at all! I believe it was a terrible mistake by an imperfect prophet. To say polygamy is from God and keep teaching it as doctrine when women and girls suffer and struggle and bitterly hate it is wrong. The whole topic is a fascinating study in psychology. We all hate it but pretend that it will all be okay someday and even try to talk ourselves into the things we might like about it. But it is sexist and wrong and hurts us in so many ways. I wish we would just admit it was a mistake.

My husband has promised me that he will not be sealed a second time. I have promised him the same. It's the only way I have found peace with this horrible part of our belief system. To me the very thought of eternal polygamy feels *exactly* like an affair, a replacement, a rival, an enemy living in my home. My feelings have not changed in fourteen years. Our church needs to know how deeply this offends and hurts us. There must be more active, temple-going, married, super-serving, awesome-on-the-outside Relief Society presidents like me who are seriously rocked because of this male-centric, sexual-based doctrine.

When I served as bishop, perhaps a dozen or more women asked me about the sealing policies and if there will be polygamy in heaven. All I can remember is how painful the conversations were. I don't remember anger, but confusion and heartache were always part of it.

My great-grandmother killed herself because of polygamy. My grandmother was raised by the first wife.

Although it seems ridiculous now, as a young woman preparing to go on a mission, I felt that the litmus test of true righteousness and obedience, at least to some degree, was *not* just to see if I would follow Jesus and be a good person—any Christian could do that—but to see if I would be generous enough to allow other sister wives to share my husband. Would I be unselfish when the time came? Selfish, after all, is one of the worst things you can call a Mormon woman. I'm glad to be finished now with the crazy-making thought that polygamy came from God.

I was so horrified by eternal polygamy—something I didn't really know about until I was an adult and engaged to be married—that I briefly considered not getting married at all, or at least, not in the temple. There were a few nights I cried myself to sleep.

Our legacy of polygamy invites doubt. Not just doubt in God, but doubt in the safety and stability of our most private, precious relationships. It suggests to women that what amounts to deep betrayal may come to us at any moment, and that our feelings of anguish would be yet another sacrifice on the altar of devotion.

When you knock, ask to see God—none of the servants.

—Henry David Thoreau

-3-

The "Why" of Mormon Polygamy

Who did it?
Where did it take place?
When did it take place?
What happened?
Why did it happen?

EVERYONE WHO HAS studied journalism—even me as editor of our little newspaper at BY High School—learned the rules of journalism. In reporting every story, the "Five Ws" had to be carefully observed. For the story at hand, the first four are pretty straightforward. There are numerous books about Joseph Smith and about Mormon plural marriage. What follows are very brief summaries.

Who did it? Joseph Smith, founder of the Church of Jesus Christ of Latter-day Saints, and eventually thousands of his followers.

Where did it take place? Kirtland, Ohio, and Nauvoo, Illinois, then later in Utah and many other territories.

When did it take place? It began in the mid-1830s, flourished underground in the 1840s, was publicly acknowledged in 1852, was an essential aspect of Mormon life for decades, officially ended in practice by two "manifestos" in 1890 and 1904, continued covertly for years, continues into the present in actual fact in the "fundamentalist breakoff groups," and continues in belief and in preparation for eternity in the mainstream LDS Church today.

What happened? Joseph introduced the principle of "plural marriage" to the church he had founded, a principle he felt he had received by revelation from God. He himself took between thirty and forty wives. His first and only legal wife, Emma, was deceived and was often furious and driven to distraction. Numerous young women (and some older women) were approached by Joseph and promised the highest exaltation in heaven—along with their entire family—if they accepted him as their husband and were "sealed" to him for eternity. Many of these marriages were consummated. Eleven of his plural wives were women who were already married to other men. It is likely that these marriages were not consummated but were rather "sealings" for eternity. Joseph taught the principle to select others and ordered them to secrecy. When word of this unusual form of marriage reached the surrounding communities, Joseph denied it. The uproar over this violation of conventional morality was a major part of what led to his assassination in 1844.

Finally we come to the last question. For the story of Mormon polygamy, the "Why" is both central and elusive. As I briefly address this subject, I will participate in two ways. (1) I will state the answers I have been given at various times, in various places and by various people, doing it as a dispassionate journalist would. (2) I will respond to that answer as a Mormon woman who has in the past been personally and deeply hurt by this doctrine.

Why did it happen? The official position of the LDS Church today is that God commanded that plural marriage commence, even sending to Joseph an angel with a drawn sword who threatened the Prophet's position and even his life if he did not obey. Later, God commanded that the practice cease.

But *why? What purpose did it serve?*

(1) It was necessary "to multiply and replenish the earth." And it helped the church to grow very quickly.

To date there are no proven progeny from Brother Joseph's polygamous marriages. And according to the church's website, "Studies have shown that monogamous women bore more children per wife than did polygamous wives except the first." Additionally, a study of the children of wealthy polygamous men and the children of poorer monogamist men in nineteenth-century Utah showed that children of the monogamist men had better survival rates. As for helping the new church to grow, polygamy likely repelled rather than attracted converts.

(2) Polygamy was needed in order to provide husbands for the large surplus of female members, especially widows.

That has proven to be unfounded folklore. According to LDS apostle John A. Widstoe, "there seem always to have been more males than females in the Church." And if there had been more women, Mosiah 21:17 in the Book of Mormon suggests an excellent remedy that did not involve marriage:

> Now there was a great number of women, more than there was of men; therefore king Limhi commanded that every man should impart to the support of the widows and their children that they might not perish with hunger; and this they did because of the greatness of their number that had been slain.

(3) Polygamy produced more *faithful* members of the church.

Heber C. Kimball had forty-three wives, with seventeen of them bearing him sixty-five children. I asked Tom Kimball, a descendant of Heber and his first wife Vilate, if he thought members of the church became more faithful because of polygamy. He responded, "No, it seemed to create fundamentalists and atheists. What I know about the Kimballs is that only two of the forty-two sons of Heber would become polygamists themselves, and my father would go around to his cousins converting them to the church because their parents were no longer Mormons. Even now, the majority of my Kimball cousins are not Mormon." Still, I would not be surprised to find that a high number of descendants of polygamists stayed very close to the church and became leaders because of their strong sense of heritage and because leaders often beget leaders. For many years in the nineteenth century, being a polygamist was virtually a requirement for leadership.

(4) There had to be a "restoration of all things."

What does this mean? Is not "love your enemy" a higher law than "an eye for an eye and a tooth for a tooth?" Why restore a lower law? In the New Testament, being "the husband of one wife" is in a list of qualifications for spiritual leadership. We have a pattern of moving forward, not backward.

(5) The Doctrine and Covenants, as given to Joseph Smith, suggests that God commanded polygamy of Abraham, Isaac, Jacob, Moses, David and Solomon in the Old Testament; why not again?

There is no documentation anywhere in the Bible that God commanded polygamy. Men having more than one wife existed in the culture of the Israelites and surrounding societies. Histories such as Gerda Lerner's *The Creation of Patriarchy* suggest that the practice of a man having "wives and concubines" developed from the concept of slavery. There are statements attributed to God in the Bible that regulate the marriage relationship, just as there are statements that regulate war and diet and dress. Moses? That he was a monogamist seems likely from the record. David and Solomon? Both met disasters through their indulgence in women. Of Solomon, who had 700 wives and 300 concubines, the Lord said, "neither shall he multiply wives to himself." Abraham? It was his childless wife Sarah who asked him to take her maid that "I might obtain children by her." Isaac? According to the Old Testament, he definitely did not have a second wife or concubine. In fact he and his wife Rebekah experienced the same trial that Abraham and Sarah did—Rebekah was barren. However, they solved it in a different way. Isaac "entreated the Eternal for his wife…and Rebekah his wife conceived."The brilliant Elizabeth Cady Stanton, American suffragist and abolitionist, wrote of biblical polygamy:

> Every infraction of the Divine law of monogamy, symbolized in the account of the creation of woman in the second chapter of Genesis, brings its own punishment whether in or out of the marriage relation…. Polygamy and concubinage wove a thread of disaster and complications throughout the whole lives of families and its dire effects are directly traceable in the feuds and degeneration of their descendants. The chief lesson taught by history is danger of violating, physically, mentally, or spiritually the personal integrity of woman.

(6) There are more righteous women than men, so more women will qualify for the highest degree of glory in the celestial kingdom where marriage is essential.

This is pretty insulting to men, I think. This bit of folklore may have sprung from many sources. One that I found was an oft-told dream or vision that was reported by Mosiah Hancock, son of Levi W. Hancock, a leader in the early church. In 1855, at the age of twenty-one, Mosiah saw the pre-mortal existence and the "war in heaven," a battle between the spirit children of God the Father, in which some followed God and some followed Satan. Hancock said of this battle that "no females took part against the Father and the Son," and consequently the Father decreed that "for every male that has kept his first estate…there are two females."

(7) **Monogamy leads to a corrupt society.** Brigham Young and other early LDS authorities taught that "the one-wife system" is a wicked arrangement and results in all manner of ills. Brigham suggested that it was instituted by the Roman Empire and has been "a source of prostitution and whoredom throughout all the Christian monogamic cities of the Old and New World, until rottenness and decay are at the root of their institutions both national and religious."

That's a lot of rottenness and decay to lay at the feet of monogamy. Nor does it fit at all with twenty-first century Mormonism's current actions of laying everything on the line in defense of marriage as a one-man, one-woman arrangement. Additionally, history suggests that Salt Lake City was not much different from other cities in regard to prostitution.

(8) **Polygamy was important for "kingdom building" on earth and in heaven and is essential for the highest exaltation in the celestial kingdom.** Both in Joseph's time and in Utah, it was understood that a man had the right and the obligation to create here on earth the foundations of an eternal kingdom. The greater the number of wives, the greater the man's exaltation in heaven. Charles C. Rich's first wife, Sara Pea Rich, wrote in her autobiography that she would never have given consent for her husband to take more wives "if I had not believed that those who obeyed the principle of plural marriage would receive a higher glory

in the Eternal World." William Clayton, Joseph's secretary, wrote in an affidavit: "From [Joseph] I learned that the doctrine of plural and celestial marriage is the most holy and important doctrine ever revealed to man on the earth, and that without obedience to that principle no man can ever attain to the fulness of exaltation in celestial glory."

We will have to wait until we get to heaven to know if this is true.

> **(9) Polygamy is too sacred for most people to understand. It is gospel "meat" and most of us can receive only "milk."** It can only be understood by those who have unusual faith and knowledge.

This, too, cannot be known until we arrive in heaven.

> **(10) Polygamy produces healthier children and thus a superior society.** Those who are more "fit," physically and spiritually, would create a superior breed, a chosen people prepared for the second coming of the Lord. There were countless spirits in heaven waiting for the right kind of bodies and the right lineage. Historian B.H. Roberts observed that race-culture was "the inspiring motive of the plural-wife feature of this revelation on marriage. It was in the name of a divinely ordered species of eugenics that the Latter-day Saints accepted plurality of wives."

Contemporary societies are more and more acknowledging that monogamy is superior to polygamy as a family arrangement. A 2013 study in Nigeria published in the *International Journal of Psychology and Counselling* showed that "there is a significant difference in the overall academic achievement of students from monogamous families and those from polygamous families" and that life in a polygamous family often compromises achievement and general well-being. An observer of strict Muslim societies wrote that in such places as Afghanistan, where rich men take more than one wife, "the inability of a young man to settle down in a family may increase the likelihood of his drifting toward violence."

Another health problem associated with polygamy is that a male is fertile much longer than a female is. Population geneticist James F. Crow writes that the "greatest mutational health hazard to the human genome is fertile older males." The degraded quality of their sperm can cause "serious problems for grandchildren, great-grandchildren and later generations." Today sperm banks generally have an upper age limit of 40 for men who donate.

In nineteenth-century Utah, older men were routinely encouraged to take younger wives. Lorenzo Snow, fifth president of the church, married the last of his nine wives, Sarah Minnie Ephramina Jensen, when she was seventeen and he was fifty-seven, forty years her senior. Through her, he fathered the last of his forty-two children in Canada when he was eighty-three years old.

Polygamy is also known to create problems with inbreeding. Salt Lake City's *Deseret News* reported in 2006 that Warren Jeffs's FLDS community, whose members were allowed to marry only within the group to keep the blood pure, were experiencing a shocking health problem. "Scientists knew of only 13 cases of Fumarase Deficiency in the entire world" until 20 more victims were identified, all within a few blocks of each other on the Utah–Arizona border. "Fumarase Deficiency is an enzyme irregularity that causes severe mental retardation, epileptic seizures and other cruel effects that leave children nearly helpless." Their IQs average about 25.

Stanley Kurtz, a senior fellow at the Ethics and Public Policy Center, concluded:

> Polygamy in all its forms is a recipe for social structures that inhibit and ultimately undermine social freedom and democracy.

A hard-won lesson of Western history is that genuine democratic self-rule begins at the hearth of the monogamous family.

In 2000, the United Nations Human Rights Committee stated that:

> Polygamy violates the dignity of women. It is an inadmissible discrimination against women. Consequently, it should be definitely abolished wherever it continues to exist.

More and more states worldwide are abolishing polygamy. LDS scholar Valerie Hudson reported that her book *Sex and World Peace*, written with three co-authors, provided data that was used by the Supreme Court of British Columbia "in their landmark decision to uphold Canada's ban on polygamy."

(11) Polygamy made certain that the church stayed in the limelight year after year so lots of people would know about us. B.H. Roberts suggested that the fact that Mormon polygamy was anathema for such a long time wherever it was known could have been a blessing in disguise. He said that it possessed "a certain publicity value to the whole work of God," keeping the message before legislatures, presidents, even the Supreme Court, and "through that court has attracted the attention of leaders of thought in all the world."

Most of us would find the notion that "any publicity is good publicity" to be suspect. What if our church had taken the road not traveled? What if we had become known, not for polygamy, but for refusing to attack when Brother Joseph was murdered—for making the desert blossom as the rose—for being a people who truly attempted to create and live in Zion and love one another and be a light to the world? How many more doors might that reputation have opened to the missionaries? And how much grief would have been avoided in terms of public relations and private pain and injury to the integrity of the church? President Dieter Uchtdorf, a member of the First Presidency today, said, "Let us be known as a people who love God with all our heart, soul, and mind and who love our neighbor as ourselves." We are still fighting the battle of being known first of all for our polygamy.

> **(12) Polygamy weeded out the less-committed members.** Elder Bruce R. McConkie said, "If plural marriage had served no other purpose than to sift the chaff from the wheat, than to keep the unstable and semi-faithful people from the fullness of gospel blessings, it would have been more than justified."

This feels like a harsh and arbitrary winnowing. One example of this "chaff" was David and Jeanette Evans McKay, a couple in Huntsville, Utah, who refused under considerable pressure to enter polygamy, yet gave to the church one of the brightest lights in its history, President David O. McKay.

(13) Except for polygamy many of us would not be here.

This claim relies on a deterministic model of the universe that Mormon theology thoroughly rejects. I am a descendant of a polygamous union. I will tell in this book of a great-grandmother on my mother's side who said no to polygamy. I also have a great-grandmother on my father's side who said yes to polygamy. But the thought that my very being depends on the establishment of Mormon polygamy relies on fatalistic reasoning that flies in the face of Mormonism's wonderful teachings about the eternal existence of souls, each with its own agency and ability to choose its own path. I'm sure that many beautiful children have been born as a result of every war that ever occurred, of rape, of all kinds of strange situations and terrible errors, none of which proves that war, rape, and terrible errors are good after all.

My eternal soul depends on no particular earthly circumstance. With or without Brigham Young pressuring my great-grandfather Joseph Wright to take Mary Ann Fryer as a young second wife so she could help him settle Southern Utah while his first wife stayed in the Salt Lake area, I would have still wormed my way into mortality and found the perfect soil for my growing. But even though, as you can tell, I personally reject polygamy as God-commanded or as a "higher" form of marriage, I honor the lives and the commitment of our ancestors who did accept what they felt was a divine call to live that order.

> **(14) God commanded polygamy in the LDS Church to try his people, just as he commanded Abraham to sacrifice his son Isaac.** Yes, the practice is unjust and sexist and hurtful, and there is no good way to defend it, but God gave it as a test of faith.

I do not believe that the God of love works this way. In the terrible story of Abraham being commanded to kill his son Isaac, the knife was raised but the sacrifice was interrupted before it was enacted. There was no ram in the thicket for the Mormons. The appalling trial of Mormon plural marriage was not interrupted decade after decade, and the painful story continues today. Isaac is spared the blow. Mormon women are not. Many have described the promise of eternal polygamy as a knife in their heart. And in these pages you will read of several of Joseph's wives who spoke of feeling as if they were called "to place myself upon the altar a living sacrifice."

"WHY MORMON POLYGAMY?" I am persuaded that any possible benefit is a penny's worth of gain for a dollar's worth of pain. And so I look further to understand the "Why" of it all. My friend Leonard Arrington was voracious in wanting to know everything about the history of our people. He served as the official Church Historian for ten years, 1972–1982, and he is credited with having created, even with setbacks, a new openness around the history of the LDS Church. Leonard loved the church and he loved honest history and he was determined that those two ought to meet in public as well as in private. I have kept a diary since 1956, and I find in those pages a conversation with Leonard dated April 4, 1973 about both his diary and mine. I concluded, "We were in agreement that truth has got to be preserved, whatever the cost."

Not surprisingly, Leonard gave a lot of thought to Mormon polygamy. The subject came up in a 2008 interview conducted by Leonard's biographer Gregory Prince. Historian James Clayton recalled:

> Once we were flying together, I think to Chicago to a historical meeting. He had been Church Historian for some time. I said to him, "Leonard, what is the most shocking thing you have found in the archives?" He waited a minute, and then spoke kind of softly and said, "The most shocking thing I have found was when Joseph Smith propositioned the wives of his colleagues, including apostles." That really disturbed him. We didn't discuss that much further, but that has now all been outlined in [Richard] Bushman's new book [*Joseph Smith: Rough Stone Rolling*] and others. But that was the thing that he found most shocking, at least initially after he had had some time in the church offices.

I find in my diary for December 9, 1972 an account that is relevant.

> The thing I remember more than anything was a comment [Leonard] made about polygamy. In an earlier interview he had said to me, "The last word has not yet been said about why the Mormons practiced polygamy." I asked him to clarify that if he could. He said that every week the church loses members to fundamentalist break-offs, and it's awkward because the things we say about them are merely the things the world was saying about orthodox Mormons before the Manifesto (men being led by the flesh; unthinking women). He and some colleagues are doing research into it.
>
> Right now he's working on a kind of a touchy [theory] that I perhaps shouldn't even put down in print, but I will…. [A] principle of adoption…existed in the early days of the church

and died out about the nineties, if I remember right. A young man, for instance, who left his family to join the church, and wanting to belong to a family unit, was "adopted" into a family—and this as an eternal sealing.... Brother Arrington feels there is a real significant key to polygamy in this principle of adoption—and he is open to the possibility that it was all supposed to have been a theoretical thing and not involve actual, consummated marriages.... I knew that Joseph had had many men sealed to him. I asked Brother Arrington in what exact relationship that had been done. "As sons," he answered.

Leonard adds to that thought in his own diary of August 4, 1972:

Hundreds of young men were adopted into the families of prominent church leaders.... I don't know of any instance of the adoption of young women. The young women were simply sealed as plural wives of church authorities, so this is how they came under the law of adoption....

This is all a very strange kind of theology—a theology which the present generation of LDS find difficult to understand. The church's attitude during the last 30 or 40 years has been to avoid mention or discussion of it, but I do not see how we can avoid grappling with this problem if we are to write honest history.

Later, during the time I was working on my screenplay about Joseph's life, I went to Salt Lake City to do some research and pick the brains of people who studied Mormon history for a living. My diary report of August 23, 1979 tells me that I had good visits and interviews with a number of people, among them my friend Leonard. Leonard knew about the film in development and was happy to hear I was working on it. As we discussed polygamy, his thoughts were very close to what he had expressed seven years earlier. He described it as an "unintended consequence" of Joseph's devotion to uniting his community in a way in which everyone he loved would be together forever. That it moved in the direction of plural marriages, Leonard felt, was simply an "unintended consequence."

On the same date I also interviewed Maureen Ursenbach Beecher, a BYU professor who had written extensively on Mormon women; Linda King Newell, who was then writing—along with Valeen Tippets Avery—the 1984 biography of Emma Smith, *Mormon Enigma*; Ron Esplin, historian working on the Brigham Young papers in the church archives under Arrington; Eugene England, professor of English at BYU; and Marvin S. Hill, then professor of American history at BYU and the author—with Dallin H. Oaks—of the award-winning *Carthage Conspiracy: The Trial of the Accused Assassins of Joseph Smith*. Regarding our conversations about polygamy, I wrote in my diary:

> [Eugene] England told me in Leonard's new book, *The Mormon Experience*, he had written polygamy from very much of a naturalistic development, but then changed it somewhat feeling he couldn't get away with it.
>
> Esplin is the only one who gives a totally divine origin of polygamy. The others allow for a considerable amount of human intervention. Hill, for instance, feels that...there is a period of time where Joseph is writing of a great anguish that he is going through. It can't be accounted for in anything that is going on at that time. Hill feels that he had fallen in love with Fanny Alger and didn't know what to do. Joseph then writes that he had found his peace. It was during this time that accounts have it that he married Fanny Alger. Also during this time Joseph is retranslating the Bible and, being in the dilemma that he was, found in the marital style of the patriarchs an answer to his problem. So he put it through his mechanism for getting revelation and came out feeling a divine sanction.

Regarding Fanny Alger, who worked in the Smith household—as did a number of Joseph's subsequent young wives—a close friend of Joseph's, Benjamin F. Johnson, recalled that Fanny was a "comely young woman" whom everyone seemed to like and that "it was whispered even then that Joseph loved her." The wording of Joseph's proposal to Fanny appears not to mention a command from God, but speaks of Joseph's desire. (The word "desire" appears in D&C 132, Joseph's revelation regarding polygamy: "... if any man espouse a virgin, and desire to espouse another....") Fanny's uncle, Levi Hancock, after receiving permission of the girl's parents, approached her, saying, "Fanny, Brother Joseph the Prophet loves you and wishes you for a wife. Will you be his wife?" Fanny agreed. A ceremony was performed by Uncle Levi, who repeated the words as Joseph spoke them. Interestingly, this occurred prior to 1836, the reported date when Joseph received the "sealing power" from a heavenly messenger.

"Error" is a really useful word. I make errors on a regular basis, as we all do. It is not possible, in the huge work Brother Joseph did, that he made no errors. LDS educator and humanitarian Lowell L. Bennion writes in *Understanding the Scriptures*:

> Some writers cover up the humanity of their religious leaders. Not so with Old Testament authors. They tell of Jacob's deception toward Esau, Isaac, and Laban, as well as his strength of character. Moses, revered as the greatest among the prophets and as the spiritual founder of his nation, takes honors unto himself that belonged to God. (See Numbers 20:10–13 and Deuteronomy 32:48–52.) And David, Israel's idyllic king who defeated the whole of Canaan in battle, is portrayed as a murderer and an adulterer—and in the end, as a pathetic old man. Saul, Israel's first king, ends his career in madness, while Solomon ends his in utter folly. In fact, most of the kings of Israel and Judah are described as having done "evil in the sight of the Lord."

Everyone whose life Mormon polygamy touches must in her or his own way come to terms with where it came from and why it happened. Many people believe that God commanded it for God's own reasons. Many people believe it came simply from Joseph's ego and his sexual desires. I believe that Joseph's personal desire clearly played a part, but I also agree with biographer Richard Bushman that "Nothing in his later life excited Joseph more than the idea of joining together the generations of humanity from start to finish," and that Joseph "did not lust for women so much as he lusted for kin." It appears that several of his marriages to much older women were contracted as a favor to one of their family members. And historians have recently become aware that, during the terrible time in Missouri, Joseph's fifteenth wife, Eliza Roxcy Snow, noted poetess and zealous leader, was a victim of brutal sexual violence that left her unable to bear children. Reportedly, Joseph took her as one of his wives to comfort her with the assurance of eternal connection and heavenly progeny. Desire—compassion—the celestial business of knitting families together to build his own heavenly kingdom— these appear to be some of the motives for Joseph's choices in his persistent matrimony.

WHEN HEAVEN HAS an earthquake you fall to your knees and feel through the rubble to find the pieces of God. When my eternal, temple-blessed marriage shattered and everything that had been meaningful lay in jumbled shards around me, I had to slowly and carefully pick up every single piece and examine it, turning it over and over, to see if it was worthy to keep and to use in building a new house of meaning. As I gathered the broken pieces of God, I used only my own authority, only my own relationship with the divine, and the good, small voice that speaks inside me, to appraise them. I threw away many, and I kept many, assembling the bright pieces into One Great Thought. I asked only, "Do I see God's fingerprints on this? Does this little piece feel godly? Does it speak of love?" That made it easy. I was forever finished with the insane attempt to love a God who hurts me. When I picked up the little piece of God-ordained polygamy, I smiled because there was no question. I thanked the God of Love, and I threw that piece away.

My CHOICE IS not between either honoring our founding prophet or acknowledging that he made a significant error. I choose both. I can love King David for "The Lord is my shepherd..." even though this is the same man who arranged the death of Uriah after taking his wife Bathsheba in adultery. Quantum physics has proven light to be at once both wave and particle. Like David, Joseph was at once both a man of God and a man of earth, and he never claimed to be perfect.

But this is the thing. No one today weeps in the night because in 1837 Joseph Smith made the monumental error of establishing the "Kirtland Safety Society," an underfunded bank that promised riches, failed within weeks, and caused financial ruin and loss of faith for a large number of his followers. Yet thousands and thousands, perhaps a number larger than we can even imagine—women and men in today's LDS Church—still live with sadness or fear, or anger and confusion, some weeping into the night because of the Ghost of Eternal Polygamy. Something went terribly wrong, and I believe that God insists, and insists very loudly, that we Latter-day Saints do everything we can to put it right. We will not leave the pain unattended. We are better than that.

And now I wonder. Those who have lived very large lives, who have left legacies beyond their deaths—do they continue to feel both the positive and the negative effects those legacies have on those who are now taking their own turn on earth? None of us wants to be remembered for our errors. None of us wants to see hurt and know that it has come from our actions. I believe that seeing Joseph's polygamy as an error is the kindest way to evaluate it. And the surest way to correct it.

Brother Joseph said that "Friendship" is a "grand fundamental principle of Mormonism." True friendship, I believe, is described in that lovely thought I have read more than once from writer Dinah Craik, who lived in England during Joseph Smith's lifetime:

Oh, the comfort—the inexpressible comfort of feeling safe with a person—having neither to weigh thoughts nor measure words, but pouring them all right out, just as they are, chaff and grain together; certain that a faithful hand will take and sift them, keep what is worth keeping, and then with the breath of kindness blow the rest away.

I count myself as a friend to Brother Joseph, and I wish to honor him like this. I hold the fullness of his life in the palm of my hand, chaff and grain together. I keep the many kernels worth keeping, and with the breath of kindness blow the rest away.

Other Voices:

"I'm looking for another home where the gospel tastes sweet again"

My wife and I married in the temple when we were both twenty-one years old. We've been married for fifteen years and now have four children. The current temple ceremony, sealing policy, history of polygamy, along with the current unclear doctrinal standing of polygamy have had a direct effect on both our marriage and our relationship with the church.

My wife, a convert to the church at sixteen, has stopped attending church after many years of struggling in good faith with the gender issues that exist there. She is a faithful, loving, truth-seeking person. She is smart and well-educated. She is empathetic and generous towards history. She wants to believe. At the root of her disaffection is not just the history of polygamy and related issues of gender inequality, but also our modern church's refusal to deal with these issues in any sort of way that looks or feels authoritative or prophetic.

The broad expansive theology of Joseph Smith resonates with her soul and mine. Yet, a truly honest, even generous, look at the history of polygamy and treatment of women in the church reveals so much coercion, inequality, and sadness. We just cannot believe that polygamy as practiced by Joseph or Brigham was a model of a God-sanctioned eternity. The current temple ceremony unequivocally places woman in a direct hierarchy with the man as an intermediary between her and God. This, as a man, makes me deeply uncomfortable.

I refuse to accept an asymmetric covenant in which my wife's promises to me do not match my promises to her regarding our standing before God. These covenants intentionally create a hierarchy, not an equal partnership. Modern efforts to correct this fall heart-breakingly short.

My wife and I have decided together that until this changes, the temple is too hurtful to attend, especially for my wife. And I will not go without her. We do this trusting that a loving God who knows our hearts will not deny us any blessings now or in the eternities for following our most deeply held spiritual promptings.

We know this makes more "orthodox" believers sad. We imagine this makes our leaders sad. However, we believe it pleases our God.

It would take revelation to change the things that we find so hurtful. I hope such revelations come. I personally believe the reluctance to seek such revelation stems from a desire to protect our priesthood leaders of many years past. I find it sad that we seem to care more about the reputation of men who are gone than we care about the hurt, suffering and pain of living Latter-day Saints.

We really wish the church the best. It has given us much in our life. However, we are literally this week deciding whether we can remain active or whether we will move on to build a life outside of Mormonism. If we do choose to stay active, it will be without temple recommends, with alternative ways of paying tithing, and with clear boundaries on how we allow the current institutional church into our lives. Much of our decision will be whether we feel we can trust our daughters to the institutional church and whether my wife can participate and maintain her mental health and personal integrity.

We know that our leaving won't change the church. We are far past believing that we can do anything to change it. Rather, the question is that we live our life in accordance with our deepest held spiritual values. We may find it better for us to live in the ever-growing diaspora of Mormon heterodoxy. Maybe that is the path God wants us to walk, the one that is healthiest for us. We know that we aren't the only ones. There are many of us. Many who stay despite these deep concerns. Many who leave because of them.

Progress is a messy business. It always has been. We each have our role to play. My ancestors played theirs. I now play mine. I wish these things didn't have to be issues for us. I wish the temple ceremony reflected equality as a value. I wish we as a people could—with clarity and revelation--get out from under the awful cloud of polygamy. For this I pray.

As I went to college and discovered I had a brain, I simply could not reconcile the LDS Church's past and current doctrine with my own growing sense of self-worth as a woman. As painful as it was to leave all of the other incredibly wonderful things about LDS culture behind, there was simply no way, for me personally, to "get ok" with the behavior of Joseph Smith and Brigham Young as it relates to women.

Furthermore, while no one in my own LDS family practiced polygamy, sexism endured and has been very destructive to every relationship between family members: parents, children, siblings. Sexism is the root of LDS polygamy. And sexism lingers on.

I remember the Sunday I learned about polygamy when I was twelve. I went home and prayed in my room for hours, all the while crying about the unfairness of it all. Fast forward many years to one Sunday at church when my twins were just four years old. Our son during sacrament asked why only boys were passing the bread. Before I could answer, he said "Oh! Is it because boys are better than girls?"

If a barely four-year-old is perceiving the inequity, I don't have it in me to fight the battle of "re-teaching" after every Sunday we go to church. So now, away from the distress our church brought to me, I am just teaching my children to live good lives, and I surround us with people of similar values, regardless of religion.

I am in the bishopric in my ward. One of our members is a man who is completely inactive because his wife is sealed to her former husband and, in the eyes of the church, the two children he had with this wife are sealed to the former husband whom they both dislike. This has been a painful thorn for them. The daughter has realized that she is sealed not to her father but to this man she doesn't even know, and she brings this up often in the Young Women's organization. No one has an answer.

It is so frustrating to me as a leader that this policy has changed entire lives for the worse and driven these good people from the church. I pray for a change that would ease the minds of so many people.

My great-grandmother was the fifth and last wife of my great-grandfather and the only one of his wives he had not been commanded by Brigham Young to marry. She was eighteen and he was forty-six at the time they married. She was beautiful, intelligent, and accomplished—and courted by men her own age. She had a long widowhood. All of this troubled me greatly when I was a young romantic myself. I loathed polygamy, even though I was a product of it.

In my former therapy practice, some of my clients were the wives of men who had "received revelation" that they were to practice polygamy. It became something of a specialty of mine. I had friendships with people who were polygamists, and I spent time in their home. I was able to see the belief in and practice of polygamy up close and personal. Nothing I saw endeared it to me; in fact, what I knew made leaving the church that much easier. Eventually, I knew too much to stay. I have seen too much of the dark underbelly of patriarchy. Especially polygamy. It is dark indeed.

My mother left the church as a means of ending a sealing that she did not want to perpetuate. Her marriage was not violent, and so she was told that she would not be supported in her decision to cancel her sealing. She loves the church, but refuses to sustain a leadership that would attempt to usurp the healing power of God in ending painful relationships.

The doctrines associated with sealings—particularly in our male-centric mode where only men are able to choose who is sealed to whom, where only men do the paperwork of sealing, where only men do the ordinance of sealing, where only men are allowed to have multiple sealings, is the chief reason that I do not consider myself completely within the community of the church.

I attend consistently and serve constantly, but I am looking for another home where the gospel tastes sweet again.

Lifelong member, served in leadership roles, gave countless hours of service to the church, served in missionary programs, etc. My wife and I left the church with our three young children a couple of years ago. Historical and current issues, a lot having to do with polygamy, plagued our minds. No answers were to be found. Mental anguish was extreme, almost clinical. Leaving the church has been a positive experience the longer we're out of the faith.

Recently I received from my bishop an email that said, "Although your permission is not required for your former husband to cancel his sealing to you and receive a clearance to be sealed in the temple to his current wife, your thoughts on this would be appreciated."

I responded, "It is fine with me. He is a good man and I want nothing but his happiness. I appreciate the fact that my permission is not required for him to be sealed to a second woman, and that is a great example of why I am no longer an active member of the church. I cannot endorse nor stand by a church with such discriminatory and gender biased practices."

Polygamy is my heritage, but, as a child, young adult, and then a wife and mother, I always knew that it could also be my future. When I began studying the history of my pioneer Mormon ancestors, I had to face head on all of my fears surrounding polygamy. I also had to face that, despite a few public statements to the contrary, plural marriage is still very much a part of LDS doctrine. Recently, I heard with my own ears one of the Twelve Apostles proclaim that he fully expected to have with him for eternity the wife he currently lives with as well as the one who passed away.

I felt overcome with grief. I had always believed in a loving Father in Heaven, who cared for his daughters as much as his sons, but everything about polygamy yelled out to the contrary. Mormon heaven would be hell for me. Soon I began to see all of the other ways the church devalues women, and I ceased to believe.

I hope that someday the church will officially disavow the concept of plural marriage and fully embrace women as equal partners with men. Until then, I find much greater peace outside the LDS Church.

As a new bishop I had a woman in our congregation who was trying to make her way back to church after years of not being active. The ward and I welcomed her and her children with open arms and warmth of spirit. It wasn't long before she requested an interview with me. When she came in to the bishop's office I could tell that she was troubled.

She told me that when she was in her early twenties her mother passed away of a sudden heart attack. She teared up as she remembered the moment she found out her mother had died. A few years later her father married another woman in the temple and she was sealed to him. Hesitantly she asked, "Is it true that my father will have two wives in the next life?"

I found myself struggling to share what I knew was the case. "Yes," I said, "according to current church practice, a man can be sealed for eternity to more than one woman."

The words seemed to fall from my lips like daggers to her heart. Her voice shook as she said, "I thought we didn't believe in or practice polygamy anymore."

At that moment, I found myself inadequately prepared and a little resentful that I had to be the one to answer these questions. What can a local leader say to ease the pain of this woman who now saw herself as part of an eternal polygamous family? I did my best but the wound was too great and the words of comfort felt hollow even to me.

A few weeks later, she stopped coming to church. Despite our continued efforts to reach out to her, she and her children never returned. Polygamy drove this sister away from a ward family that loved her.

The woman's cause is man's—they rise or sink together.

—Alfred Lord Tennyson

-4-

I Will Tell Emma

VERY HIGH ON my list of people I hope to visit with when I get to the other side is Emma Hale Smith, first (and only legal) wife of the Prophet Joseph. Brigham Young told me I would have to go to hell.... Well, he didn't directly tell me to go to hell, but in regard to finding Emma he wrote:

> ...[S]he will be damned as sure as she is a living woman. Joseph used to say that he would have her hereafter, if he had to go to hell for her, and he will have to go to hell for her as sure as he ever gets her.

I'm pretty sure Brigham was wrong about this. He missed the boat on a number of things. Brigham didn't like Emma. He didn't like uppity women. I, on the other hand, love uppity women and believe we need a lot more of them.

Actually Mormons don't really have a "hell" where you are forever in torment (except for that handful known as "sons of perdition.") Everyone else will eventually find themselves in a really good place. I believe that I will be able to seek out Emma. One of the first things I will tell her is that, in spite of what Brigham said, the LDS Church today has a very high regard for Emma Smith, honoring her tremendous work and sacrifice and position as an "Elect Lady."

I then want to put my arms around her and tell her I have moaned in empathy for the hell that she was put through on this earth. I picture her greeting me outside her heavenly, homey cottage with its vast and colorful garden—a cottage that can turn into a castle whenever she feels like it. I picture her a strong and glorious woman who smiles as she welcomes me.

Just now I printed out a picture of Emma and taped it on the wall so I can see her face above my computer screen. It's the "official portrait," the only picture of her that I really like. She is not quite smiling, but she is beautiful with dark ringlets on the sides of a well-formed oval face with large dark eyes and a good straight nose. She wears a white lace shawl. She looks regal. In her other pictures she looks very old and very sad.

I'm sure Emma smiled in her youth. Especially when she was young and with Joseph. She was in love, and when you're in love you can't stop smiling. Emma's love for Joseph was such that this uppity woman eloped with him after her father had several times rejected Joseph as a suitor. It was 1827. Emma was twenty-two years old, five feet and nine inches tall, skilled in guiding her canoe on the Susquehanna River, confident riding her horse. More educated than most women of her time, she was known for her quick wit and her independence. Joseph was a year younger and less educated than Emma, having had only two years of formal schooling, but his powerful, charismatic presence and penetrating blue eyes won her.

I like to imagine them out in the sunlight riding their horses, singing one of the songs of the era, maybe this bluegrass folksong that was like a tennis match with constantly changing rhymes lobbed back and forth:

Will you wear blue, my dear, O my dear,
Will you wear blue, Jennie Jenkins?
Yes, I'll wear blue, for I know your love is true...

I believe their love was true, was ardent and passionate and respectful. And in the days before the strange development that turned their marriage on its head, I think they were happy together. In spite of the trials brought by poverty, by being driven from place to place, by the stresses of what they both saw as Joseph's large and prophetic calling, they were happy together.

And then came the great and terrible revelation. Joseph was no longer hers alone. God had called him to do what some prophets did in that long-ago sandy, windy world of camels and turbans and tents—take plural wives. The first such event was five to seven years after their marriage and was with Fanny, a comely young woman who worked in their home, a "transaction" that Emma saw with her own eyes. She and their friend Oliver called it "adultery," but Joseph called it "celestial marriage" or "the new and everlasting covenant." Enter, polygamy, present in the flesh. And Emma Smith was the first woman in its path who wept.

> Will you wear grey, my dear, O my dear?
> Yes, I'll wear grey, my trust he did betray...

There are so many things I want to tell Emma. I will tell her that I walked where she walked in Nauvoo, Illinois, as I attended a leadership conference for Affirmation, an unofficial support organization for LGBT Mormons. I hope I won't have to explain that acronym to her. Joseph taught that we grow eternally in light and understanding, and I believe Emma will be up to speed on whatever I have for her. I'll tell her how I loved walking out by the Mississippi River, just a short distance from the "Mansion House" that she and Joseph finally were able to call home after unbelievable sacrifices. How I stood on the river bank right where she would have stood and I picked out of the water a brown seed pod the size of my palm, one of thousands floating down the river and sitting now on my desk as I write. How I had an unexpected and wonderful experience "presenting Emma" to sixty or seventy Mormon gay men and women upstairs in the "big room" of Joseph's Red Brick Store, all of them deeply moved to learn more of this woman who had experienced profound hurt at the hands of a church she loved, just as they had.

I think she will smile at the mention of the store. The "big room" was the place in which she and her Mormon sisters met in 1842, after they had been organized under the direction of Joseph as the "Relief Society," a service organization that Emma, as president, soon began to use in her fight against polygamy, an organization that was consequently shut down by the brethren shortly before Joseph's death. Emma was learning the devastating truth about her husband. By the end of 1843, Joseph had taken between thirty and forty wives, some already married to other men, some sealed to him only for eternity, but many sealed for both time and eternity, including a traditional, marital, sexual relationship. Evening comes. Where is Joseph? Midnight. Where is Joseph? Emma's mother-in-law Lucy was the only woman in Nauvoo whose relationship to Joseph was without question. Anger. Words. Tears. Emma's arms, strong enough to guide her canoe through the Susquehanna, were not strong enough to beat against Joseph and God. Her eternal exaltation was at stake. She gave in, took women by the hand and gave them to Joseph. She watched as the two Partridge sisters were married to her husband, not knowing it was a charade to appease her, not knowing that they had been married to him months before. Then almost immediately she rose in defiance and ordered the women from the house. Less horrendous things have driven women mad. Emma railing against Joseph and God.

> Will you wear red, my dear, O my dear?
> Yes, I'll wear red, he is in another's bed...

I WILL TELL Emma that my empathy for all that she went through is real, tell her about that freshman English theme I wrote—"A Fate Worse than Death—Polygamy." I will tell her my story, pitifully small compared to hers. Life plays such strange tricks. Ironically a form of polygamy came knocking at my door. Not my front door, my back door. My gay husband Gerald never wanted a divorce. He wanted a non-monogamous marriage, and his pleas were passionate. "Loving two, three, or four people does not take away from loving one," he said. "I want you, I want our marriage, but I want, I must pursue this other need. It will never go away. Can't you try?"

"I can't, Gerald. I've played it over and over in my mind. It's not possible. I can't."

I had watched Gerald's excitement as he told of discovering a group called "Gay Fathers" and started going to their weekly meetings. Getting ready. Trimming his blond.mustache. Tucking in his plaid shirt. Putting on cologne. Humming.

I watched. A little bit like Emma. Enough to be able to say to her that I come with a heart full of empathy.

Will you wear brown, my dear, O my dear?
Yes, I'll wear brown, for my world is upside down…

Emma's love and my love were swept into an ungovernable current. Joseph's wife watched, helpless, as that current became a force that led to her husband's death. The same was true for me.

OF COURSE I will tell Emma about the women two centuries after hers, who lived their lives in the resounding echo of grief that she experienced, who lived their marriages with fear like hers. Women whose husbands or teachers read to them the same bitter words from the revelation that Joseph's brother Hyrum brought and read to her, causing her to implode with grief and explode with anger.

"And let my handmaid Emma Smith receive all those that have been given unto my servant Joseph…and if she will not abide this commandment she shall be destroyed, saith the Lord…" (D&C 132:64). Thousands of women, receiving what they believe to be a message meant for all women, suffer their own version of the grief of Emma Smith. Joseph is dead. Brigham is dead. But the Ghost lives on.

I especially want to tell Emma about my experience in the Red Brick Store after I had finished my presentation about her in the "big room." I was the last to leave. Downstairs on the first floor was a reconstructed country store that sold a variety of things reminiscent of those that would have been offered in the 1800s. At the counter was Lachlan Mackay, a member of the Community of Christ (formerly the "Reorganized Church of Jesus Christ of Latter Day Saints," the main branch of the Mormon movement that refused to follow Brigham and stayed in Nauvoo with Emma and her family). Lachlan had been our very engaging guide as we walked through several of the Smith properties, and he knew of my interest in Joseph's polygamy. I was now his last customer and I brought to the cash register several items to purchase, including a glazed mug featuring raised artwork that says, "Joseph Smith's Red Brick Store" (now a treasure on my desk that holds pens and scissors and powerful memories). I thanked Lachlan for graciously staying a few minutes overtime for me.

"Happy to," he said, as he carefully wrapped my things for travel. "You know," he went on, "right upstairs is the office where Joseph wrote down the section in your Doctrine and Covenants about plural marriage."

I stared at him. "Right up there? That's where Joseph wrote down Section 132?"

"Right up there."

"I—I have to go back up for a minute. Please."

"Take your time."

I hurried up the stairs. "It's the room on the right," Lachlan said.

There was a velvet cord across the entrance. I called down, "I'm going to go inside. I won't touch anything."

"Go ahead."

I unhooked the velvet cord and entered the room, lit only by the light from the stairwell and the moon out the window. A desk. A couple of chairs. Other items from the period. I stood, amazed at being there. I was quiet for a couple of minutes just breathing and feeling. I called up the memory of that day, July 12, 1843, and watched the well-documented events unfold. There were three men in that office—Joseph, his brother Hyrum, and his secretary William Clayton—discussing plural marriage and Emma's refusal to accept it. I listened as Hyrum urged Joseph to write the revelation down and let him take it over to Emma and read it to her, certain he could convince her it was of God. Joseph replied, "You do not know Emma as well as I do." Hyrum persisted, and so Joseph spoke the revelation, which William wrote down sentence by sentence.

I walked with Hyrum as he hurried to his sister-in-law, sat in her home and read aloud the revelation that spoke of the eternal nature of the marriage covenant and the acceptability, sometimes the commandment, of plural marriage. I watched Emma's face, only skeptical at first, become hard, her eyes narrow, her mouth pursed as she heard the words directed to her, "...but if she will not abide this commandment she shall be destroyed, saith the Lord...."

I watched Emma rise, now with fire in her eyes, as she angrily ordered Hyrum to leave, saying that those words were not from heaven but had come straight from hell. Hyrum left. Emma collapsed in sobs, and I watched, seeing it all as I stood there in Joseph's office in the Red Brick Store.

I remembered then the "big room" just feet from where I now stood. I watched as Emma and her Mormon sisters, in that room, in their homes, in their wagons, in sickness and trial, in childbirth, welcomed and used the spiritual power Joseph had promised them. They administered to one another through the anointing of oil and the laying on of hands. They rebuked illness and darkness. They pronounced healing blessings and did so in the name of the Lord.

A strong intent moved through my body and settled in my chest. I raised my palms in front of me and I spoke aloud, softly.

Dear God, our Father and Mother who art in heaven and in our hearts and in this room. I am so grateful to be standing here. I am grateful for the beautiful and important things that happened in this city and in this building. And now as a member of the church that Joseph founded—as a Mormon woman who has been blessed by many things that happened here but has been deeply wounded in consequence of something that transpired in this room—I take it upon myself to pronounce a healing blessing.

I bless the hurt that has developed from some of the words that were written in this room, words in what is known as Section 132 of the Doctrine and Covenants, words that through many generations have harmed the hearts and lives of countless Mormon women and men—that this hurt will have an end, that the damage done by the concept of eternal polygamy will cease, that the wrong will be righted, and that soon there will be a time of new light, of healing and of peace. Through the power of my love and my faith I pronounce that this blessing will be fulfilled and I do it in the name of Jesus Christ, amen.

I WILL TELL that story to Emma when I visit her in that better place we look forward to. And then I will ask her to walk with me to the Peering Window designed for us to see mortality. We will look at the large and beautiful world our Divine Mother and Father created together and peopled together, and we will locate there the smaller world we both knew, the Mormon world that was seeded with Joseph's vision. I hope and I believe that we will see a good and honest and quirky people still striving to build Zion, finding deserts to make blossom as the rose, men and women happily pioneering in partnership, no Ghost of Polygamy to hurt or make afraid.

Other Voices:

"If God didn't care about Emma's feelings, he certainly won't care about mine"

When I read in the Doctrine and Covenants about how Emma Smith was threatened that God would destroy her if she did not accept polygamy, I realized that if God didn't care about Emma's feelings, he certainly wouldn't care about mine. This led to depression and anger. I secretly hated God.

When my husband and I read the Doctrine and Covenants section about polygamy for what was to be our last scripture study, I wept and wept. It had been a long time since I had read that section all the way through, and it was as if a curtain had fallen: I clearly saw the harm in this principle. Poor, damned Emma! Nothing makes me feel more like a chunk of property than being something that the Lord gives to a man on account of his righteousness.

I can say definitively and with relief that my fear and angst went down precipitously after my husband and I left the church. Additionally, my perception of my body immediately became more positive, and my marriage, which was wonderful even before we decided to leave, is now better than ever. We can truly have an equal partnership now, and we preside equally in our home. My desires matter just as much as his do. I have not felt such deep, resounding peace in a long, long time.

God's cruelty in the Old Testament feels disconnected and general, but the cruelty to Emma Smith (and me) in D&C 132 is personal and biting. Emma would be destroyed if she did not support Joseph's desires. I don't believe in a cruel God. Joseph's introduction of polygamy spawned the horrific evils of Warren Jeffs and the like, and I feel ashamed to have any connection to it, distant as it may be. Polygamy is the smoking gun that destroyed Mormonism for me.

When I told my dad how the scriptures about polygamy really hurt me, he told me that if I were more spiritually mature polygamy would not bother me. From that point on, I always doubted my own feelings about it being wrong and assumed it was a lack of personal faith and an inner rebellion that kept me feeling so raw and angry about it. Through the years it put a major strain on my faith and kept me from ever really being able to experience the other elements of the gospel that might have brought me the joy and peace that I so much yearned to feel.

I tried my hardest to stay in the church, but eventually it was impossible, and polygamy was always at the root.

My grandfather is sealed to two women. My mother came from the first marriage, and this has caused enormous torment in her family. I taught Doctrine and Covenants in seminary the year we married in the temple, and was horrified to realize the import of Section 132. It was under this fear that I married, and I have agonized over it for thirty years.

My daughters have chosen not to be married in the temple, in part because of this issue. My female friends who remain sealed to former spouses in spite of their ex-husbands' behavior, are left in the ridiculous and impossible position of trying to move on with their lives while remaining eternally sealed to these men. As true believers, they can't move on.

It is humiliating and demeaning. Sometimes frankly I'm comforted that my daughters no longer have to agonize over this as I have done.

By my senior year in high school, the knowledge that women were eternal chattel was a thorn wedged deeply into my soul. The adolescent female psyche is a fragile thing. It doesn't take much for a young girl to feel bad about herself. I had become completely convinced that marriage was not something to look forward to, but rather the kick-off to a future of being owned by my priesthood-holding, exaltation-bound husband who would marry other women who would join my eternal marriage in the afterlife.

If a fraction of a doubt about the eternal aspect of polygamy existed for me at that point, it was shattered by my seminary teacher. He said earnestly, "God did tell Emma Smith that she would burn in hell if she did not accept polygamy." It was there in black and white in D&C 132. I left class that day in tears, and I never went back.

I felt that my only option was to marry a priesthood holder in the temple or not marry at all. So, I decided at a very tender age, perhaps only nineteen or twenty, that I would never marry. That decision was incredibly destructive in my life. I descended into a very dark depression. I no longer cared what happened to my life. I tried to have professional goals but I had no determination to pursue them. For the most part, I just didn't care if I ever did anything with my life. In the darkest, worst part of my depression there were days when the only human interaction I had was with a teller at a bank or saying "excuse me" as I passed someone in a store.

Then my story changed. I met a wonderful man who used to be LDS. I decided that Heavenly Father would accept that I simply couldn't live up to the standards of the celestial kingdom and it would be OK that I never humbled myself to accept polygamy. It would be OK that I ended up a servant or in a lower kingdom. In that moment, I freed myself! I could do whatever I wanted! Build whatever life I wanted! Never mind eternity, I was going to figure out how to be happy in the here and now!

My depression evaporated. My life became colorful and interesting. I saw a worthwhile future for myself. I am now happily married and—even though I mourn the decade I lost to the myth of eternal polygamy—I count my many blessings and look for ways to help those who are less fortunate than me.

A number of Institute teachers at the University of Utah were absolutely insistent that polygamy was required for exaltation, and they made sure we knew it. You could just feel the tension and apprehension in the room! Section 132 of the D&C—especially the "be destroyed" part—was drilled into us. We women specifically were told that our monogamous views were simply a product of our culture, and that, once we were on the other side, our eyes would be opened and we wouldn't have any problem with it. Bludgeon is the right term. I have felt bludgeoned with polygamy!

I was sixteen years old when the man who was taking me home from a babysitting job asked me if I'd ever read D&C 132. It was a long ride home, and by the time we arrived at my house, I had received a proposal and a strict instruction to keep his lecture secret. (I can't call it a conversation, I didn't say anything.) He was comfortable enough with the ideas he was spouting that when we got to my house he tried to kiss me.

When I got into the house, I was still so shaken from fighting him off that my parents could tell something was wrong. And that's what saved me. I poured out the whole sordid story to them. My dad told the man that if he contacted me again he would break his face. About a year later, another young teenager took him up on his proposition. When that happened, our small Utah town shunned the family until they left.

I caused the widow's heart to sing for joy.

—Job 29:13

-5-

Is There No Help for the Widow?

THE PROPHET JOSEPH SMITH was a Mason. Many prominent men of his time joined the Masonic Order, and when Joseph joined he rose rapidly to become a Master Mason, as did many of his brethren. On that terrible day of June 24, 1844, when Joseph and his brother Hyrum were murdered by a mob, as the Prophet fell from the second-story window of the jail, his anguished cry, cut short, was the first four words of what was known as the Masonic "Grand Hailing Sign of Distress"—"Oh Lord my God, is there no help for the widow's son?" Without doubt there were some Masons in the attacking mob, bound by oath to assist a brother who gave that cry, but there was no help for Joseph.

Not long ago, as I stood in that upstairs room in Carthage, Illinois, looking out the window from which Joseph fell, I was deeply moved. I wished that I might have heard his cry, and I wished that I might have provided some help. Today the help that I feel called to give is to my Mormon brothers and sisters whose poignant cry has reached me—not help for the widow's son—but help for the widow herself.

For centuries in many Asian communities, "no help for the widow" led to her committing suicide by fire, throwing herself on her husband's funeral pyre, a barbaric ritual known as "suttee," now illegal internationally. We prefer the sensibilities of nearly all of our religions in which caring for the widow is required by God. "You shall not mistreat any widow or fatherless child" (Exodus 22:22). "Religion that is pure and undefiled before God, the Father, is this: to visit orphans and widows in their affliction" (James 1:27). "The one who looks after and works for a widow…is like a warrior fighting for Allah's cause" (Muhammad). In the Book of Mormon, Nephi repeats word for word the Lord's admonition in Malachi 3:5, "And I will come near to you in judgment; and I will be a swift witness against…those that oppress…the widow and the fatherless…" (3 Nephi 24:5).

The Mormon widow faces a uniquely difficult circumstance not faced by a widow in any other religious community. There are many complexities and some confusion in the "sealed" and "formerly sealed" relationships that may occur in Mormondom, but to understand the painful stories of many women and men, the essentials are these: if an LDS man wants to have an eternal relationship with the woman he marries and have an eternal relationship with the children he fathers, it is of primary importance that he marry a woman who is available to be sealed to him and not one who has already been sealed. To understand how this came about requires a walk back into history.

ON THE DAY the Prophet Joseph was assassinated, between thirty and forty women became widows. I have no doubt their mourning for their prophet-husband was deeply sincere. They all revered him, likely loved him. Some of these women lost Joseph as their "celestial only" husband and continued to live with their "for time on earth" husband. But I believe that for all of them the relationship with Joseph held great meaning. Suddenly the Twelve Apostles, the leaders that inherited Joseph's mantle of authority, had the welfare of his many wives to consider.

Thus was born a Mormon version of a "levirate marriage," which is an arrangement mandated in the Bible (Deuteronomy 25:5–6) obliging the oldest surviving brother of a man who dies childless to marry that man's widow, with the firstborn child seen as that of the deceased brother and not of the genetic father. There was an understanding regarding the subsequent marriages of the wives of Joseph that is essential to know in order to comprehend the dilemma of today's Mormon widows and the men brave enough to marry them. All of Joseph's wives—eventually even those who were married "for time" to their first husbands—were sealed to Joseph "for eternity." This meant that the women themselves and any children they birthed by their first husbands, as well as any children they would subsequently birth by the husbands who claimed them after Joseph's death, belonged to Joseph in the next life as part of his eternal progeny. Brigham, Heber, and the other men became "proxy husbands" to Joseph's widows and evidently felt honored to assist in building the eternal kingdom of their friend and prophet, acting as "proxy fathers" to the children that were thus sired.

Todd Compton's comprehensive study of the wives of Joseph, *In Sacred Loneliness*, tells that

> Brigham Young, Heber C. Kimball, and the rest of the Quorum of Twelve Apostles approached the widows of Joseph Smith and offered themselves as husbands. Smith reportedly had asked the apostles to do this if he should die.... Brigham married between seven and nine of them; Kimball married approximately eleven.... Prominent church leaders in Nauvoo...married others.

Lucy Walker Smith, who was given to Heber C. Kimball, wrote:

> The contract when I married Mr. Kimball was that I should be his wife for time [on earth], and time only, and the contract on the part of Mr. Kimball was that he would take care of me

during my lifetime, and in the resurrection would surrender me, with my children, to Joseph Smith....

A CLOSER LOOK at one of Joseph's plural wives will help to fill in the picture. Zina Diantha Huntington Jacobs Smith Young is one of the most accomplished women of early Mormondom. In 1841 in Nauvoo, Zina was courted by Henry Baily Jacobs, described as "a handsome, articulate twenty-three-year-old who played the violin" and was a staunch, committed Mormon. During the courtship with Henry, Joseph proposed to Zina, teaching her the principle of plural marriage. Zina was understandably shocked and, unlike many of the women to whom Joseph proposed, she refused him in favor of the man she loved. Joseph had agreed to perform the marriage ceremony, but he did not show up, and so the marriage was performed by someone else. Joseph later explained that God had told him Zina was to be his celestial wife and he could not give away that which was his.

Even after Zina's marriage, Joseph continued to approach her. After a fourth proposal—in which Joseph told her about the angel with a drawn sword, and told her that he was commanded by God to claim her as his wife—Zina, seven months pregnant, did agree to be sealed to Joseph "for eternity" while remaining still married to Henry Jacobs. After Joseph's death, Zina—now pregnant with her second child by Henry—agreed to be sealed to Brigham Young "for time," still with the assumption that she would continue to be the wife of Henry.

One of my closest friends for decades is a descendent of Zina and Henry. In one conversation he told me, "All the Jacobs family that I know of, we assumed that Henry must have been a bounder and that's why Zina left him. And then we discover that *Zina never left him, that Henry faithfully served a number of missions on which Joseph had sent him. And that Henry was also away serving a mission to England on which Brigham had sent him when Brigham persuaded*

Zina to actually live with him as a wife!" Later Zina bore a child by Brigham.

Publicly Henry appeared to give consent to this spiritual advancement for his wife, despite the wrenching loss it meant for him. Evidently he felt, concerning both Joseph and Brigham, that "whatever the Prophet did was right." However, my friend has given me copies of letters Henry sent to Zina over many years pouring out his loneliness and his ongoing love and yearning for her. "And to the end of her life," said my friend, "Zina's true love was Henry. In her diary, Zina wrote every year, 'Henry's birthday.'"

I recall the sadness in my friend's voice as we discussed what looked like an injustice done to a good man who was devoted both to his wife and to the teachings of what he accepted as the restored gospel that included plural marriage and the privileges of authority. "Is it the understanding of the posterity of Henry and Zina," I asked, "that in the eternities all of you belong to the eternal kingdom of Joseph Smith and not of Henry Jacobs?"

My friend said quietly, "Yes. We don't understand it, but we feel like everything will be worked out justly in the eternities."

When powerful men of elite status take more than their share of wives, there are obviously not enough women to go around. Many of the less powerful males have to be sacrificed on the altar of attaching attractive women to those who are believed, by themselves and by the community, to be higher on the scale of spiritual authority. Henry Jacobs was always faithful to the church, but was for a time excommunicated by Brigham Young, reportedly as a result of Henry's ongoing attempts to win Zina back. Finally Henry did remarry, evidently at Brigham's strong suggestion, but always he yearned for Zina, his first and only love.

I AM NOT able to trace precisely how the handling of the problem of Joseph's many widows became codified in later Mormon policy, but the result of it has profound effects on three groups of LDS people today:

(1) A widow who has been sealed to her deceased husband is understood to be part of the eternal kingdom of that husband and consequently is not generally seen as a desirable choice by men who are looking for a wife. (In recent years, a woman's descendants may have her posthumously sealed to all of her legal husbands if all parties are deceased. The clear understanding is that in heaven she will choose one of them as her eternal husband. It is possible, but not guaranteed and is often very difficult, for a woman to get a "cancellation of sealing" regarding a deceased husband. The subsequent situation of that now-single husband in the eternities is painfully unclear. The stories included in this book testify to the confusion that surrounds this subject.)

> When a Mormon guy told me—"If we were to get married, it would be my duty to do all that I can to help you obtain the celestial kingdom so that you can be reunited with the husband you're sealed to. So in essence, it would be my job to make sure you leave me!"—I guess he was right, that's what we're taught. But there's something really, really wrong with this. Sort of like adding salt to a wound.

(2) A man who marries a sealed widow is understood to serve the purpose that Brigham and Heber and the other church leaders served for Joseph, to care for the woman "for time only" and relinquish her in heaven to her first husband.

> At BYU I ran into a girl who I had known and liked in high school. I thought of asking her out, my mind already wondering if she might turn out to be "the one." However, as we talked more I learned that she had gotten married in the temple soon after high school, but that her husband had been killed in an accident only a few months after her marriage.
>
> Immediately I realized that I was not interested in dating or marrying her because I would not want to love her knowing that she would be given to another man in the hereafter and that I would be left alone and probably in a lesser kingdom.

(3) Children who are born into a marriage between a sealed widow and a new husband, though these children are raised by their biological father, are understood to be destined to live eternally in the spiritual kingdom of a man they have never known but who has a patriarchal right because of the prior sealing.

> My grandmother lost her first husband in World War I. After the war, my grandparents met and raised a family of five children. My dad, who was very close to my grandfather, told me that Grandpa was deeply burdened and many times in tears over the fact that his five children were not sealed to him. He was taught and believed that his children were sealed to Grandma's first husband and he would lose his own children in eternity.

LONG AGO, IN the lives of the men who became temporary custodians of Joseph's eternal wives and temporary biological fathers to Joseph's eternal children, there would not have been the danger of everlasting loss that there is in the LDS Church today. In mid-nineteenth century, the men who took on such a task had an advantage of circumstance that LDS men do not have today—polygamy as a practical, immediate option. In addition to the children fathered with Joseph's widows as a favor to the Prophet, Brigham and Heber had plenty of wives who were sealed to them alone, and plenty of children who came from these wives, thus building their own robust eternal kingdoms at the same time that they were advancing the kingdom of Joseph. They did not experience the risk or the sacrifice faced by Mormon men today who have only one wife. According to current policy, if that wife is sealed to someone else, the man faces an eternity without wife and without children (even those born with his own DNA), unqualified for the highest blessings of the celestial kingdom.

The pain of this circumstance—to the sealed widow, to the man she might marry, to the children they may have together—can be extreme. There are those who offer balm in the words, "Well, Heavenly Father will work things out. He wants us all to be happy." That is small comfort in the face of what are presented in the here and now as absolute doctrine and policies that come directly from God. The stories I have received from those affected by these policies break the heart. These are my sisters, the Mormon widows for whom a heavy blow is added to a terrible grief. These are my brothers, the Mormon men with the love and the courage to marry a sealed widow, believing that it may place them at eternal disadvantage. Our Mormon community is better than to be comfortable with this injustice, and I believe that soon we will craft a response that will be for our widows not an affliction but a blessing.

Other Voices:

"Being an LDS sealed widow is sort of like being a leper"

I know an LDS widow who told me, "A man at a single's event actually left me on the dance floor, saying, "I can't dance with you, you're a widow." And even worse was when I was on a church singles' cruise and the first night at dinner a man said to me when I told him I was a widow, "What are you doing here?—You're no good to any of us." Being an LDS sealed widow is sort of like being a leper. Makes me pretty angry that church leadership doesn't seem to care much about this.

What organization discriminates against widows—and also penalizes the men who choose to marry them? Only one that I know of—the Mormon Church. I am aware of three cases that dramatically demonstrate this.

In a tragic accident, ten people were killed, most of them LDS. Here, in brief, are the stories of three people who lost loved ones in that accident.

A young man had been engaged for one week to a young woman who was killed. He easily received permission to have her sealed to him in the temple by proxy. Not long after, he married a woman and had her sealed to him as well, insuring that he could claim them both as his wives in heaven.

Two women that I personally know, then in their twenties, lost their husbands in that same accident. One, over the years, has found it impossible to find an LDS man who would accept her status as a sealed widow, and has determined to live the remainder of her life alone.

The other woman, after much frustration and rejection, found a wonderful LDS man who married her knowing that she would not even attempt the difficult process of getting a sealing cancellation as she felt it would strip her deceased husband of his eternal exaltation. They love each other, but she has confided to me that LDS doctrine and sealing policies have continued to cause great heartache and pain for them both, that their unsealed status is the elephant in every room, making them (and members of their families) feel like their marriage is "less than." Her husband has said he feels like a place holder and is faced with the reality that under LDS theology, he will not be with his wife and biological children hereafter. He spoke of a recent Sunday School lesson that labeled all marriages that were not sealed for time and all eternity "counterfeit" marriages. The pain is excruciating, and he is left wondering how a merciful and loving God can be behind such a plan.

Who is discriminated against in these three stories? Certainly not the man who easily was able to start building his eternal kingdom with his two wives.

As a single mother I raised my children in the church and supported my two sons on missions. My oldest son, who all of his life has been an active, worthy member of the church, is married to a wonderful woman who was widowed (while pregnant) at age twenty-one. They now have two children together, who are not sealed to their own father but to a man they don't know. My son's heart aches to be a part of the eternal family that he was always promised by the church he believes in.

He now feels his mission was wasted by teaching people they could be with their families forever. He can't, and for no fault of his own.

I have a friend whose sister was widowed young. She had a hard time remarrying a Mormon because Mormon men wanted women who were unsealed. She did eventually find someone, and then went through hell trying to get a cancellation of the sealing. It was a humiliating process, and included getting letters of permission from her former husband's parents. She sort of had to drag that husband, whom she had loved, through the mud to prove that the sealing ought to be cancelled.

After a woman goes through the terrible process of cancelling a sealing with a first husband who died (assuming that cancellation is allowed, which many are not), I have to think—what about the first husband? Our doctrine states that he is still very much alive on the other side of the veil, yet he had no say in this decision, and now he is sealed to no one and supposedly loses his future of exaltation. Who wins in all this?

If the sealing policies were reversed and men had to live for years in loneliness until they happened to find a widow they could marry for time only, do you think that these policies would even exist? Of course not!

On my second date with "Jane" I was at her apartment for the first time looking through her record albums. I noticed a name on many of them that wasn't hers. I asked her who "Richard" was. There was an awkward silence and then she asked me to sit down because she had something important to tell me. Later I learned she was sure I would be one more man who would be moving on from her life.

We sat on the couch together as Jane related her brief marriage to her husband Richard some four years prior. How they had loved each other, had believed he had beaten his cancer and so had moved ahead and were sealed in the Idaho Falls Temple. How nearly all of their eleven months of marriage was spent in the University of Utah Hospital while he went through chemotherapy before he finally passed away.

As if the death of Richard wasn't bad enough, Jane then had to deal with moving on into the dating world and found that her sealed status made the possibility of marriage in the temple to a good active LDS man seem quite remote. Several men that she had become serious with were not able to overcome their fear and concern over their eternal status. Not wanting to be one more suitor to develop a relationship with her and then leave, I told her I would take some time to study and pray about this the rest of the week and get back to her.

I found little in LDS writings to give me hope regarding my eternal status if I did marry her. In his book *Doctrines of Salvation*, Joseph Fielding Smith said that becoming an angel was the best I could do instead of moving toward godhood as we are taught to aspire to. Of course D&C 132 didn't offer much hope either. And yet my sense of God's character was such that if I felt impressed by the Spirit to marry Jane, how could he punish me for doing so? The God I had come to know was merciful, just, kind, and compassionate—all the things that his son Jesus exemplified. If I can't trust this God, who can I trust? So after prayer, fasting, study, and discussing it with my parents, I decided to move forward with the relationship.

Jane and I have been happily married for thirty-two years. Several years after our marriage, we had two biological boys and adopted a two-and-half-year-old girl. The boys, of course, are sealed automatically to Richard and Jane. Michelle, adopted, is a floater—we never did figure out a way to explain to her that her only chance to be "sealed" was to a man she never met.

I guess I kept hoping the policy would change. I pursued that several times with different temple presidents who offered hope that it might, but it didn't. Their suggestion was always that Jane have the first sealing cancelled. Neither Jane nor I ever felt right about that. Richard was a good man. I've written a number of letters hoping for a policy change. The answer is always no.

My argument has always been, if we truly believe in a God who is just, merciful, compassionate, fair, an equal opportunity exalter—then why not let my wife and other women be sealed to more than one man and let God work it out in the next life? Surely he can work it out to everyone's satisfaction—this *is* God the Almighty we are talking about!

At this stage, I'm not so sure about all this individual family fiefdom building. So where has all of this taken Jane and me? Still in love and with our family still loving one another. At this point, I'm the only one who still fully believes in the church. Jane doesn't care for the temple, isn't so sure about the church in general, and hasn't attended for a number of years. Our two boys and their wives are devout atheists but good people. Our wonderful, unsealed, adopted daughter is something of a Buddhist. We all get along well and there's lots of love to go around.

I've come to believe that whatever the question, love is the answer. It may sound simplistic and it is. But it's really deep and broad—broad enough to cover this whole temple policy thing if we would let it. God does the love thing really well. It's the forte of our Heavenly Parents and their good son Jesus. And finally it's the only thing that really matters.

My brother died at the age of twenty-nine, leaving a young widow and a two-year-old daughter. After a few years his widow was planning to marry a man who had never been sealed. My family was a neighbor to a member of the Quorum of the Twelve Apostles. The couple asked him whether or not they should marry. He said under no circumstance should this man marry my sister-in-law because he would be denied exaltation.

It seemed crazy to me that if a man is willing to make a family and raise my niece and help my sister-in-law in this life that God would hold it against him. They did not listen to the General Authority and got married anyway, but it has caused feelings of concern and doubt and may have been part of the husband eventually choosing to become inactive in the church.

After I noticed how young some of the second wives of the General Authorities looked, I wondered if this had anything to do with current temple marriage policy that widowers can be sealed in the temple to second and third wives, but widows cannot. So I did some research.

Every single General Authority in the last thirty years who remarried after his wife died chose a never-married (and much younger) woman, with the exception of one, whose second wife was divorced from a man who had left the church, and she received a sealing cancellation before this second marriage.

It seems to me that the General Authorities really, really believe in eternal polygamy and that's why they themselves aren't marrying widows. And all we hear from them is "don't worry about it."

My husband "Mark" and I have made numerous attempts to get permission for us to be sealed without requiring that I break the sealing with my deceased former husband. Shortly after we received a letter from the secretary to the First Presidency denying that request, Mark was able to get a hold of him by telephone.

The secretary was very short and seemed bothered to have to speak to Mark. When Mark asked whether our letters had been read in their entirety by the brethren themselves he responded, "Do you not believe the brethren to be inspired?" He showed little compassion or empathy.

Mark said, "I am really struggling with how to explain this policy to my children, to tell them they are sealed eternally to a man they have never known."

The response was, "Well it all goes back to your decision to marry a sealed widow." To every question Mark asked came the answer, "Again, it all goes back to your decision to marry a sealed widow."

Mark said, "I find it offensive to hear you say that."

The secretary responded, "Well that is just the way it is. You can ask your wife to cancel her sealing and then be sealed to you and that is all that can be done."

Mark said he knew of examples in the historical record that proved there had been exceptions to this policy and that allowed a living sealed widow to be sealed to a second husband. The secretary responded with "Well, I would like to see that!"

Mark asked if he could email him these accounts. The response was "You can send them to me, but I don't believe it will change their answer."

Mark emailed him the examples, and the secretary never wrote back.

However, our bishop informed us that our stake president had received a letter regarding us from church headquarters. The bishop came over and read it to us, but would not give us a copy. It was written after the secretary brought to the First Presidency the materials Mark had sent to him. The letter explicitly stated that because I had said in my letter that

I was not going to cancel my sealing with my first husband, the consequence was that I could not be sealed to Mark. It said that I could do one of two things—change my mind and have the first sealing cancelled or wait until we both die and have our heirs seal us together. It directly stated that at some point, whether in this life or the next I was to make a choice as to which husband I want to be with for eternity.

I feel very little hope after this. Are church leaders truly aware of the difficulties their policies place on women who lose their husbands? Clearly they are clinging to the preservation of eternal polygamy. Are they aware of the problems that idea causes in a marriage? They blame Mark for marrying me in the first place, and then they blame me for not wanting to cancel my prior sealing. All this feels so inconsistent with the God I believe in. Our bishop feels that this policy will change and that we should not lose hope. But how far into the future? And what about the pain that is going on today in countless homes?

Mark has now determined that the LDS Church has no authority over what goes on in heaven regarding relationships or anything else. He no longer attends, and he now feels more at peace about our marriage.

God will be very cruel if he does not give us poor women adequate compensation for the trials we have endured in polygamy.

—Mary Ann Angell Young,
legal wife of Brigham Young

-6-
The Celestial Law

MARY COOPER AND James Oakey, my maternal great-grandparents, married in 1840 and settled in Nottingham, England. Victoria was on the throne, and occasionally the citizens of Nottingham came out to pay honor as the queen in her carriage passed through on the way to Belvoir Castle. Mary gave birth to seven living children. James became a designer and maker of lace and also helped to develop new lace-making machinery.

I have brought up from the fireplace mantle to sit beside my computer while I write a framed four-inch square of delicate Nottingham lace, a product of James's work, precious enough to cross the Atlantic and to cross the great plains. The lace is black, a color all citizens wore in 1861 mourning the loss of the beloved Prince Consort Albert.

In 1850, the Oakey family was baptized, joining the more than 33,000 Latter-day Saints in the United Kingdom and Ireland (compared to 12,000 in Utah at that time). Missionaries, enthusiastically preaching on street corners and in homes, had reaped a fruitful harvest since their arrival at Liverpool in 1837 with their optimistic gospel of new revelation from God, a restoration of lost truths, and a vision of a people preparing for the return of the Lord. For some time James and Mary maintained the mission home in Nottingham, the center of the work for all of England. James became branch president, then district president.

Like most wholehearted converts, James and Mary were anxious to gather to the new world and be part of this high endeavor, and by 1862 they had gathered the necessary funds. As they packed the very few things they could take on the voyage, my grandmother, eight-year-old Sarah, was told that none of her large collection of dolls could go. This story was repeated to me often as I grew up:

James said, "We all must make sacrifices, Sarah. And your dolls will be your sacrifice for Zion."

"Father, what is Zion?" Sarah asked.

"Zion, my darling, is the pure in heart."

According to the story, Sarah sadly but bravely dressed and arranged her much-loved dolls around a little table and told them goodbye.

MARY AND THE children set out for the six-week voyage on the *John J. Boyd* numbered with 701 Saints of like disposition and destination. James was to make as much money as he could and follow as soon as he was able. One daughter, determined to stay with her boyfriend, abandoned ship just as it was to sail. Another daughter died of mountain fever as the family crossed the plains in a covered wagon. As little Sarah walked the 1300 miles, and as the wagons creaked their way west, they left behind them a nation playing out the bloodiest battles of the Civil War.

Their company reached the Salt Lake Valley on October 1st, 1862, making their way through Emigration Canyon, where the oak, maple, and aspen trees were aflame with the red and orange of autumn. Fifteen years earlier, in 1847, Brigham Young and the first company of Mormon pioneers had arrived and entered a semi-arid valley whose major attraction was that nobody else wanted it. The

Mormons had been evicted from their homes in Illinois by mob violence and were determined to become a nation unto themselves. Brigham had inherited the mantle of the prophet from Joseph Smith, and he was committed to bringing to fruition Joseph's vision of Zion. By the close of the 1860s, 80,000 converts had made the trek to the Utah territory, and the wasteland was truly blossoming as the rose.

My friend Church Historian Leonard Arrington wrote in his biography of the man who was the mastermind of it all:

> Brigham Young was a kingdom builder with dreams as grandiose as Sam Houston or John C. Fremont. But unlike them, he was successful.... Brigham Young was the supreme American paradox...the business genius of a Rockefeller with the spiritual sensitivities of an Emerson.... He was not merely an entrepreneur with a shared vision of America as the Promised Land; he was a prophet...and he built beyond himself.

By the time my great-grandmother Mary and her children arrived in the Salt Lake Valley, it was far different from when Brigham had first gazed on it and famously said, "This is the place." I wonder if Mary even believed her eyes as she looked down from the rim of the valley into a basin that was thriving. And that large building there—that adobe Grecian Doric building with pillars at its entrance looking as if a tornado may have brought it in from some far-off land—looking like it might be—a theatre! It was true—a theatre in the desert, completed and dedicated in March of the same year that Mary and her children arrived. Along with his keen sense of business and colonizing, Brigham brought across the plains his love of the finer things of life.

In the dramatic company that Joseph had organized in Nauvoo, Brigham performed in the romantic tragedy, *Pizarro*, playing an Incan High Priest, a part that some said he played for the rest of his life. Even before the temple was completed, Brigham insisted on building what became the Salt Lake Theatre, a showplace that quickly became a national landmark, seating 1500 people in a spacious hall with two balconies, galleries, boxes, lit by countless candles, elegant chandeliers and suspended coal oil lamps, featuring a deep stage with a wide drop curtain and professionally painted backdrops. Mormonism attracted not only lace makers, but architects, painters, glaziers, artisans, and builders of all kinds. The first play was *The Pride of the Market*, one of the eighty in the repertoire of their already developed theatre company. It was said that there was no star of the American stage who did not make an appearance in this remarkable venue. Years later, a non-LDS author went so far as to declare that the Salt Lake Theatre was "one of the Seven Wonders of the theatrical world." Perhaps my great-grandmother managed to bring her children to the theatre, bartering for tickets with eggs, cheese, vegetables, or doilies.

As a drama student in the university named after Brigham Young, I memorized his remarkable statement: "If I were placed on a cannibal island and given the task of civilizing its people, I would straightway build a theatre for the purpose." And now, writing this book, I feel compelled to mention the theatre to give more soul to the story of the Mormon people and to underline my intense admiration and appreciation for Brigham Young and all that was accomplished through him. Brigham was far, far more than a man who had fifty-five wives.

STILL, THERE WAS *that*. Polygamy. Brigham had sent out a call to the traveling Saints to bring with them "starts" and seeds of every kind—sometimes stuck in potatoes to keep them viable crossing the plains. And prominent among the seeds that Brigham himself brought from Nauvoo to be planted in the West there was *that one thing*—the thing that Joseph had restored at the insistence of God, who had sent an angel with a flaming sword, the thing that Brigham had first resisted and then came to enthusiastically accept, the thing that was part of what brought down his prophet-friend—Joseph's vision of plural marriage.

Such marriages had continued unabated since Joseph's death but were still protected with secrecy. Here in the territory of Utah, they were finally safe. Brigham could unpack this unusual doctrine of his beloved Joseph and teach it and live it openly under the clear blue western sky where they were accountable only to God.

On August 29, 1852, under the direction of President Brigham Young, the first public acknowledgement of Mormon polygamy was made. Apostle Orson Pratt spoke in the Old Tabernacle to a crowd of perhaps 2500 people on the necessity of the plurality of wives as

> a part of our religion, and necessary for our exaltation to the fullness of the Lord's glory in the eternal world...to raise up beings...that are destined, in their times and seasons, to become not only sons of God, but Gods themselves....
>
> I think there is only about one-fifth of the population of the globe, that believe in the one-wife system; the other four-fifths believe in the doctrine of a plurality of wives. They have had it handed down from time immemorial, and are not half so narrow and contracted in their minds as some of the nations of Europe and America, who have done away with the promises, and deprived themselves of the blessings of Abraham, Isaac, and Jacob.
>
> [The great and noble ones] are to be sent to that people that are the most righteous of any other people upon the earth; there to be trained up properly.... This is the reason why the Lord is sending them here, brethren and sisters. The Lord has not kept them in store for five or six thousand years past, and kept them waiting for their bodies all this time to send them among...the fallen nations that dwell upon the face of this earth...they will come among the Saints of the living God... [and] have the privilege of being born of such noble parentage.
>
> Now, let us enquire, what will become of those individuals who have this law taught unto them in plainness, if they reject it? I will tell you: they will be damned, saith the Lord God Almighty.

Incidentally, Elder Pratt's first wife Sarah eventually left him, left the faith, and became a strong opponent of the practice of polygamy. She called her husband's venture into plural marriage "sheer fanaticism," particularly when at age fifty-seven he married his tenth wife, a girl of sixteen. Sarah and all of Pratt's wives and children struggled in poverty.

JAMES AND MARY Oakey were still in Nottingham when that historic announcement was made—that polygamy was a true and godly principle—and only two years into their membership in this new church. A few months later in December, Joseph Smith's revelation on plural marriage was read in Britain and was met with shock and, for some, with apostasy. Likely Mary, as she began to hear the rumors validated, would have felt as did Hannah Tapfield King, who wrote to her non-Mormon brother upon hearing the doctrine of plural marriage announced at the semi-annual meeting of the Norwich Conference:

> Oh!—Brother, I shall never forget my feelings!!! It had an extraordinary effect upon me, for though I had known for a year that such a principle existed in the church, when I heard it read, and some things in it which I did *not* know, I confess to you I became skeptical and my heart questioned with tears of agony, "did *this* come from God?"

Later Hannah did come to believe the doctrine was of God, as she became the last and fifty-fifth woman sealed for eternity as a wife to President Brigham Young in 1872, five years before he died. And whatever James and Mary Oakey felt about the authenticated rumors, it did not stop them from making plans to join the Saints.

By the time Mary Oakey and her children arrived in the Territory of Utah in 1862, the doctrine was deeply planted and very well known. Many hundreds of statements by the highest leaders of the Church make clear the essential nature of polygamy as a foundational part of the gospel, such as this one by Heber C. Kimball, first counselor to President Young: "You might as well deny 'Mormonism,' and turn away from it, as to oppose the plurality of wives."

It was also clear by the time my great-grandmother arrived that not all was well in Brigham's Zion regarding this principle. He was having a difficult time getting the Saints on board, especially the women. A daughter of Jedediah M. Grant, right-hand man to Brigham Young, notably said, "Polygamy is alright when properly carried out—on a shovel." The same women that historian Wallace Stegner called "incredible" Brigham now labeled "whiners."

At a general conference in Salt Lake City in 1856, four years after the first announcement, Brigham said:

> It is frequently happening that women say they are unhappy. Men will say, "My wife, though a most excellent woman, has not seen a happy day since I took my second wife;" "No, not a happy day for a year," says one; and another has not seen a happy day for five years...many of them are wading through a perfect flood of tears....
>
> But the first wife will say, "It is hard, for I have lived with my husband twenty years, or thirty, and have raised a family of children for him, and it is a great trial to me for him to have more women;" then I say it is time that you gave him up to other women who will bear children. If my wife had borne me all the children that she ever would bare, the celestial law would teach me to take young women that would have children....

Brigham told the women he would release them from their husbands, release them to leave the Territory. But if they chose to stay,

> You must bow down to it, and submit yourselves to the celestial law.... Remember, that I will not hear any more of this whining.

IT IS POSSIBLE to find occasional stories of polygamous families who lived in some contentment. Making the best of a difficult situation is a Mormon characteristic. A culture of polygamy had become a given, rather like the weather. In Leonard Arrington's diary he gives an assessment of Utah polygamy in general:

> Nearly every important Mormon entered into plural marriage and in nearly every instance the first wife, though formerly giving her approval for the second marriage, privately opposed the second marriage and privately was jealous of the second wife. While she attempted to sublimate her feelings, these were recognized by her children and these were magnified by them so that it was impossible for them to look upon the second wife and second family in an objective way—as the children of a brother or sister would look upon aunts and uncles and cousins.
>
> Feelings developed between first, second, and subsequent families. Privately, not publicly, they made snide remarks about their "aunts." Wives would tear pages out of husbands' diaries that referred to the other wives and family. They would destroy letters to or from the other wives and families. Bitter complaints would be made which were passed onto children and great-grandchildren.

I recall those wise and piercing words of Maya Angelou: "I've learned that people will forget what you said, people will forget what you did, but people will never forget how you made them feel." That is the indisputable test of all our teachings, our doctrines, our policies. Mormon plural marriage was enacted with the widespread understanding that the Saints were preparing for a heaven in which each man rules his family kingdom, a kingdom that is more potent and more prepared for eternal increase with every wife that is acquired. Such polygamy—whether fact or fear—becomes a sanctified plundering of the position of women and of the feelings of women, robbing us of our power, our dignity and our self-respect. How Mormon women were made to feel under the trial of past polygamy and feel still under the fear of polygamy future is something that we have never looked in the face. It is a sad face. It bears some resemblance to the face of Emma Hale Smith. We must look without flinching if institutionally we are to heal.

The forced dichotomy between public presentation and personal feelings pointed out by Leonard Arrington added a second layer of awfulness to the situation: emotional inauthenticity, which I believe to be something we Mormon women continue to deal with today. In 1882, Phebe Woodruff, first wife among seven to Wilford Woodruff, fourth president of the Church, speaking at a mass meeting of Mormon women held in defense of polygamy, said:

> If I am proud of anything in this world, it is that I accepted the principle of plural marriage, and remained among the people called "Mormons" and am numbered with them to-day.

However, a few days later a long-time friend asked:

> How is it Sister Woodruff that you have changed your views so suddenly about polygamy? I thought you hated and loathed the institution.

Phebe responded:

> I have not changed. I loathe the unclean thing with all the strength of my nature, but Sister, I have suffered all that a woman can endure. I am old and helpless, and would rather stand up anywhere, and say anything commanded of me, than to be turned out of my home in my old age which I should be most assuredly if I refused to obey counsel.

Interestingly, Phebe's husband, President Wilford Woodruff, is the man who issued the "Manifesto" in 1890, which officially ended the church's support of plural marriage. This document came, not in response to the feelings of Phebe and other women, their decades of bitter unhappiness, but in response to the fact that the church faced disfranchisement and federal confiscation of its property including the temples, which would in essence destroy the church as an organization. And also, of course, so Utah could be considered for statehood.

There is no clearer evidence that plural marriage was firmly held as an essential doctrine of the Mormon Church through the four decades prior to the Manifesto than a particular formal letter that was sent from church headquarters in December of 1891. This letter, sent jointly from the First Presidency and the Quorum of the Twelve Apostles to U.S. President Benjamin Harrison, was a plea for amnesty for church members who had practiced polygamy prior to the Manifesto, members who had suffered arrests, trials, fines and imprisonment. The fifteen-man leadership wrote:

> To the President of the United States:
>   We, the First Presidency and Apostles of the Church of Jesus Christ of Latter-Day Saints, beg to respectfully represent to Your Excellency the following facts:
>   We formerly taught to our people that polygamy or celestial marriage as commanded by God through Joseph Smith was right, that it was a necessity to man's highest exaltation in the life to come.

Those words leave no doubt that, in the minds of the highest leadership and in the minds of church members, "polygamy" and "celestial marriage" were one and the same, and that the practice was essential for the truly faithful. It would be statistically impossible for all men to practice polygamy, but, according to the church's official website, "Probably half of those living in Utah Territory in 1857 experienced life in a polygamous family as a husband, wife, or child at some time during their lives." Polygamous families were considered "elite" and polygamous men were almost always those chosen for advancement in church leadership. This "elite" status influenced even later generations. A friend of mine, writer Andrea Moore-Emmett, who was not a descendent of polygamists, says, "That omission in our pioneer family ancestry always caused my mother great regret, since, according to her, it meant fewer blessings bestowed on all succeeding posterity."

ENDING POLYGAMY (which didn't really end until 1904 and even later) brought its own set of problems. One of the ironies of Mormon plural marriage is that so many women suffered deeply because it began and that so many women suffered deeply because it ended. Two sad bookends to this strange and costly experiment. Let us not forget the women who were virtually thrown to the wolves when the marriage they had been promised was God's will for eternity was suddenly in shreds.

My friend Reed Abplanalp-Cowan sent me the story of his great-great-grandmother. Melvina was a second wife, immediately resented by the first family, and when the federal government began to enforce anti-polygamy laws, she and her children were sent away from the Provo area to a plot of land owned by her husband in the desolation of the Uintah Basin. When her husband William visited his family there, he was caught by the law and sent to prison for six months. After that, Melvina and her children were truly on their own, barely surviving. Years later, when she was notified that the first wife had died, Melvina was able to move back to Provo, and she hoped her troubles had ended. But soon her husband became ill with Bright's disease, was bed-ridden for two years, and died. The children of the first family, who had always resented the second family, were now legally in charge of the estate and left Melvina with only a very small plot of unproductive land.

Her thirteen year-old Enoch, now the man of the family, wrote in his journal: "Picked at the ground all day. We are starving to death. Must get seeds in the ground and water to the seeds before fall comes. By high noon, hit more rocks than dirt and just put my head in my hat and cried and cried." The strain of so many years of bitter heartbreak and lack of help or even of food drove Melvina to a nervous breakdown, and she was committed to a mental hospital where she died. The death certificate, a copy of which I have seen, says in bold letters: "Cause of death: Exhaustion of the Insane."

BACK TO THE story of my great-grandmother. Mary Oakey and her children stayed for a year with friends in Salt Lake City and then spent a year living in a dugout in nearby Kaysville. When James rejoined the family, they were called by Apostle Charles C. Rich to settle southeastern Idaho. The little town of Paris was their destination, close to the beautiful and placid Bear Lake in a valley covered with wild game and overrun with meadow grass. James, the lace maker, turned his hands to creating bedsteads and chairs. Mary made a home from whatever was available. They were building Zion, home of the pure in heart, and sacrificing for the glory of God.

Despite evident pressure, the Oakeys appeared not to be interested in participating in polygamy. Between their arrival in Paris in 1865 and a fateful, heart-breaking event of 1873, James and Mary Oakey lived the monogamous life they had signed on for. Although there is no written record of such, there must have been conversations between this couple, and James—as an upstanding and capable man—would likely have been invited by the leadership into the order of plurality. A strong influence would have been Charles C. Rich, who presided over the entire Bear Lake region, a man who himself—back in the days of Nauvoo and Winter Quarters—had taken six wives. Rich had stayed with the Oakeys while he was a missionary in Nottingham, and Mary and her children had resided for a time with his first wife Sarah when they arrived in the Salt Lake Valley.

I can easily imagine some conversations between James and his priesthood leader, Elder Rich, based on the general documented discourse of the day. Here is a scene that might have taken place in the sawmill owned by Rich. Perhaps the two men spoke as they were cutting and grinding and sanding benches for the chapel:

"Well, James," says Charles. "President Young is putting it pretty plainly. A man who wants to rise in this church—a man who wants to rise in the celestial kingdom—that man will enter the holy order of plural marriage. I do feel to encourage you in this, James."

James is silent a moment, then speaks. "I just don't know if this teaching is correct, Charles. It doesn't—it doesn't feel right somehow."

Charles stops his work and looks James in the eye. "Do you have a testimony of the gospel, James, of the Prophet Joseph, of the restoration?"

"I do. You know I do!"

"Then trust the leaders, James! I'd surely hate to leave you behind. We are creating a *chosen people*! Enlarge your posterity! Your *eternal kingdom*!"

James shakes his head and looks down at the sawdust on the log floor. "But my Mary. How could I hurt her like that?"

"You are her head, James, her head and her God. We are the new patriarchs, Abraham and Jacob, ruling over our families with kindness but with strength! Don't fail your family, James!"

But James said no.

Perhaps the following year another conversation occurred as the two men walked together on a sunny day to priesthood meeting.

"James, last week I had to release a bishop from his position—it would not do to have a monogamist presiding over those who are living the principle."

James does not respond. Charles continues. "You should be a bishop, James. And even higher. Why, in England, you were one of our best leaders."

James slows his gait and frowns. "But I—I love Mary. She is the only one I want to be with."

Charles stops walking, turns to his companion and places a hand gently on his arm. "James. Listen to me. You can love others. As I do. It becomes a maternal love. The brethren say, 'Love your wives. But not too much.'"

James begins to walk again, quickly, as if he might outdistance the pain. "Every time I think of hurting my Mary like that—I just can't, Charles. It would break her. She might even—leave."

"James!" Charles speaks sharply. James turns and looks at him sadly. "James," the voice now is gentle. "If you do not act, your Mary—and you—may lose your eternal crowns and inherit a lesser kingdom!"

But James said no.

One more conversation I fantasize. The two men speak as they work together in the grist mill.

"Charles…I've spoken again to Mary. She says no, never. She says she would rather be damned than let another wife into the family."

Charles pauses in his work. "I am so sorry, James. Obedience. Obedience! That's the winnowing. Separating the wheat from the chaff, just like we're doing here in the mill." Charles reaches into a bushel and thrusts a palm full of kernels in front of James. "Are you wheat or are you chaff, James?"

James sits down on a stool and puts his head in his hands.

Charles continues. "I wish Mary could see, as did my first wife. A second wife is not an intruder—she is the key!—the very key to opening the door of salvation in the celestial kingdom not only for herself, but for her husband and for his first wife. If you love Mary, lead her into righteousness."

"She will not be led."

"Then you are released from the law of Sarah, my friend. You have given your Mary the opportunity to approve. She has refused. You are now at liberty to proceed. And if Mary continues in her stubbornness, she is the transgressor." Charles squats beside his friend and places a hand on his knee. "But believe me, James, Mary will become reconciled. I've seen it time and time again."

Still James said no.

And then something happened that turned the world of James and Mary upside down.

Of all tyrannies a tyranny sincerely exercised for the good of its victims may be the most oppressive.

—C. S. Lewis

-7-
No Wife at All

I HAVE KNOWN since May 30, 1972, the general story of what happened. I found the account in my diary. Married for six years and the mother of three children, I wanted to learn all I could about the family history, so I spent the day with Aunt Mamie, the older sister of my mother Emeline who had passed away when I was in high school. Aunt Mamie had brought to our home in Provo, Utah, pictures and genealogy sheets.

All she knew of what happened in the Oakey family in 1873 was very sketchy. Later I quizzed other relatives, anyone I thought might shed more light, but all anyone seemed to know were just the bare facts. Again I am going to take dramatic license and construct a scene that might represent those facts.

IT IS TWILIGHT in the two-room log cabin of the Oakey family in Paris, Idaho. The three children who still live at home—Alfred, 24, Sarah, 19, and Hyrum, 14, sit at the table reading or sewing by the light of the coal oil lamp. Mary, whose hands are always busy, mends a quilt that covers her lap. There is the sound of horses and a wagon. A muffled voice calls the horses to a stop.

Hyrum closes his book and looks up expectantly. "Father's home!"

Mary places the quilt on the chair and opens the door, letting in the chill of an early October evening. In a moment James enters, slowly. He takes off his hat and looks around as if he's not sure where he is.

Sarah stands and takes a step toward him. "Father?" she asks gently. "Are you ill?"

"No. No, I'm…fine."

Mary touches his arm. "Sit down, James."

"In a moment…a moment." James glances at the closed door and then back to his family. "I have something to tell you all. I brought someone with me…from Logan." He looks at his wife. "We knew her many years ago in Nottingham."

Mary blanches, reaches for the chair and slowly lowers herself into it.

James continues, anxious now to conclude his news. "Ann. I told you she had come over, Mary. Now a widow…she's in the wagon. I was counseled…by priesthood authority." He pauses, then speaks evenly and solemnly. "Ann was sealed to me in eternal marriage yesterday in the temple of the Lord."

The children stare at him. No one speaks. With difficulty Mary stands, walks to a coat rack, and takes down a heavy shawl.

"Mary, what are you doing?"

"What I told you for years that I would do. From this moment, James, I am no longer your wife. Tonight I will stay with Sister Olsen."

"But it is the will of the Lord!"

Angrily Alfred stands, nearly upsetting the table, and steps toward his mother, helping her with the shawl. "Mother. I will take you there."

"Mary!"

James and the other two children watch in disbelief as Alfred pushes past his father, opens the door, and escorts his mother out into the night.

THAT'S AS FAR as I imagine the scene.

What we know for certain is this. In the year 1873, directly after James came home with a second wife, Mary, his wife of thirty-three years, left him and never lived with him again. Mary took the three children who were still living with them and moved about seven miles away to a place then called Dingle Dell, now called just Dingle. She told James he was not to follow them. This is the town in which my own mother, Emeline Sirrine, was born. A history of Dingle that can be found on the Internet says: "The first permanent family came in 1873. They were Mary Oakey and her sons Alfred and Hyrum and daughter Sarah."

For the first year they lived—as they had in Kaysville—in a dugout, and then in a log cabin with a dirt floor, built by Alfred and Hyrum. Mary, now age fifty-eight, lace maker's wife from a comfortable residence in England, homesteaded 160 acres—and this in a land of dry farming...wheat and alfalfa...hawks and ground squirrels and sage hens...blow snakes and owls...winter occasionally reaching 45 degrees below zero...snow drifts that covered the fences...scarves wrapped around faces leaving an opening only for eyes. To Mary, all of this a preferable choice to living with a husband that, to her perception, had betrayed her.

In the words of Mr. Stegner, incredible indeed.

Aunt Mamie always wondered why? "Why did Grandfather take this woman as his wife? What did he see in her? Grandmother was so lovely and dainty, always wore a white apron and a black velvet cap. And this other woman—well...." Aunt Mamie would shake her head. "I'll never understand it."

I thought that I would never understand it either, and I thought there was no more information anywhere that would leave some better clues. But then—out of nowhere—the final piece of the puzzle just landed in my lap. I was listening to an episode of Lindsay Hansen Park's very impressive "A Year of Polygamy" podcast. In the one hundred podcasts in this series, Lindsay had already covered the Kirtland and Nauvoo periods, the establishment of plural marriage in Utah, and was now examining the pressure that was brought to bear on the men to enter this principle. Suddenly I heard something that made me stand frozen at the kitchen sink. "In 1873, Brigham Young gave a sermon in Paris, Idaho, in which he said that if a man refused to take a second wife, in the eternities he would lose the wife he had." *Paris, Idaho? 1873?* I rewound the sound and listened again. *Paris, Idaho! 1873!* "*...he would lose the wife he had!*"

I was thunderstruck and felt anger rising in my throat. *How could you say that, Brigham Young! How dare you say that!* I called my four siblings and told them this new piece of family history. They too were very upset. My brother Warren in St. George, Utah quickly got on the Internet and found the very sermon.

As I READ the precise words of that sermon today, I imagine another scene. This one takes place just a few weeks prior to the scene in which Mary leaves her husband, and it provides what I am confident is the missing information that explains the mystery. I place myself there in the bowery, a large open structure with a hardened dirt floor with wooden posts holding up a roof of thatched brush and willows. The population of the town is just over 500 and nearly all are present for this event. I stand just behind and to the right of President Brigham Young, and I place Mary and James and their children on the front row so I can see them. They are in their Sunday best, James wearing a dark suit, grey vest, and black bow tie, Mary in her crinoline dress and black velvet cap. Fans occasionally flutter against the heat and the flies. All eyes are on their prophet-president, who has come to give them the word of God. The sermon starts well:

The Gospel of life and salvation that we have embraced in our faith, and that we profess to carry out in our lives, incorporates all truth.... I am here to give this people, called Latter-day Saints, counsel to direct them in the path of life...[and] I have never given counsel that is wrong....

Brigham touches on many principles that I appreciate. And then—

Joseph received a revelation on celestial marriage...a great and noble doctrine.... Now, where a man in this Church says, "I don't want but one wife, I will live my religion with one," he will perhaps be saved in the celestial kingdom; but when he gets there he will not find himself in possession of any wife at all.

I look out at the front row. Mary Oakey raises her eyebrows and looks unblinkingly at her prophet. Brigham goes on.

He has had a talent that he has hid up. He will come forward and say, "Here is that which thou gavest me, I have not wasted it, and here is the one talent," and he will not enjoy it, but it will be taken and given to those who have improved the talents they received, and he will find himself without any wife, and he will remain single forever and ever.

James drops his head onto his chest and presses his fingers into his brow.

But if the woman is determined not to enter into a plural-marriage, that woman when she comes forth will have the privilege of living in single blessedness through all eternity.

Son Alfred, sitting next to his mother, reaches over and takes her hand. Mary does not flinch. James breathes deeply, looks up at Brigham, whom he now can barely see through his tears. Finally, sadly, James knows what he must do.

President Young finishes his sermon and says amen. The congregation echoes amen. I glance now at the small block of delicate lace here on my desk, the work of the hands of James the lace maker, black lace to mourn the death of the queen's beloved consort. I mourn now, too. I mourn the death of the bond of love and trust my great-grandparents had created together. I used to blame James, but now I mourn for him. He acted not from love but from fear: God's wrath is a harsh thing to fight. And I mourn for Sister Ann, the new wife. She also was directed by authority, she went, and perhaps she suffered as well, knowing that her presence broke hearts. I mourn, too, for President Brigham Young. He thought that he was never wrong.

ONE LAST NOTE to this story. A couple of years ago, my brother Warren suggested that he and I take a road trip up to Bear Lake to visit the old family stomping grounds in Idaho. I readily agreed. Our first stop was the lake. You drive around a bend—and suddenly there it is, a beautiful stretch of blue in what appears to be a desert. We then drove into the little town of Paris. The major feature in Paris is a very impressive tabernacle, built by the Mormon settlers and now on the National Register of Historic Places. Skilled artisans had set their hands and hearts to creating something of beauty, stability, and usefulness. The building is a Romanesque structure made of red sandstone that had to be transported by wagon or sled from a quarry eighteen miles away. The designer was prominent architect Don Carlos Young, one of Brigham's sons.

It is not possible to walk unimpressed through this building that can hold two thousand people. And if you have ancestors who likely helped in the construction of it, there is an added layer of appreciation. I walked down an aisle of the main hall toward the choir loft, pipe organ and podium, my hands enjoying the polished pine wood of the benches, each of them an original from the late 1880s. Very likely my great-grandfather James helped to cut and to sand some of these benches. My brother was busy taking pictures. Suddenly I said, "Hey, Warren. Would you take a picture of me up at the podium?"

"Sure."

I climbed the stairs and arranged myself at the heavy, carved wooden podium and looked out at a most amazing view, the intricate woodwork of the ceiling, the stone carvings, the balconies, and the stained glass window in the far wall. The hall had been designed by a shipbuilder from England and looked and felt like a huge and elegant hull. It was evening, nearly closing time, and the hall was empty except for my brother and me.

This uppity woman suddenly realized—*The hall was empty!*

I later realized that it had been 140 years ago to the very month since Brigham had given his fateful sermon in the bowery very close to this spot. Hundreds of Mormon prophets and General Authorities had spoken right here. I shouldn't.... But...I planted my feet, grasped the edges of the podium, surveyed the empty hall and began.

"Dear brothers and sisters. We are gathered here today in honor of my great-grandmother, Mary Cooper Oakey, who in the year 1873 had the good sense and courage to say no to polygamy. I believe you know her story—it is printed there on the program. Sister Oakey, we honor you. I am also pleased to let you know that new light has come on that troublesome subject of polygamy, new light that makes it clear that there was a lot of misunderstanding and a great deal of unnecessary pain. Hopefully before long we will be able to write 'the end' to the sad story of Mormon plural marriage. There will now be refreshments and celebration in the foyer. Thank you."

I scanned the hall again. It was still empty. But in my mind I saw two figures sitting on the front bench, one in a dark suit with a grey vest and black bow tie, and one in a crinoline dress with a black velvet cap. They were holding hands.

Other Voices:

"It no longer feels like a 'higher law' to me"

One of my great-grandfathers was a high-ranking leader in the LDS Church. He had three wives, and my grandfather was one of his children. As Grandpa played in the garden, an old man walked up the path to his front door. Grandpa ran in the house and said, "Mama, who is that funny-looking man coming up the path?" She replied, "Why, that's your father." My great-grandmother spent her days raising children and doing temple work—endless temple work. Then she died.

My other great-grandfather was also a church leader and was forced into polygamy by those above him. It broke his first wife's heart and damaged the children for a lifetime. The son born of the second marriage was never acknowledged or included as a family member. He was sad all his life about it. Both great-grandfathers served time in prison for polygamy and all of the families suffered. I am old now and all of it makes me sad and angry. I was raised to feel superior because of this rich heritage, and now I am just ashamed.

My grandmother lived in a polygamous home in Mexico (Colonia Juarez). It was a terrible situation for all three wives. No one loved the husband, and he wandered from home to home like a nomad.

When I read the journal accounts of some of my ancestors and Brigham Young's and Joseph Smith's wives, I was deeply troubled at how painful their experiences were. I feel that all of those early Saints merely turned off their own moral compass and obeyed. When reading their own words, I expected to find conviction. Instead, I found capitulation.

There is a story in my family history of a first wife refusing to be buried near her polygamous husband because she wanted no part of polygamy in the next life. I believe polygamy caused one of the biggest problems ever in our church, and its repercussions continue today. I come from a polygamous family who fled to Mexico to live in peace from U.S. marshals. My great-grandmother wrote a book depicting her life in this practice. It was horrendous and heartbreaking for her to live, and was hard for men also. It nearly killed the church.

My mother told me stories passed down from her mother, who knew people who practiced polygamy, and she said the only family where it worked at all was one in which the two wives got on well with each other and disliked the husband. I've read a lot of books about polygamy, and I have yet to hear a polygamy story that sounds remotely like the sanitized concept of polygamy as it is taught in church.

I am a descendent of Ellis Reynolds Shipp, one of the first female doctors in Utah. Brigham Young sent her to Philadelphia to attend medical school, leaving her children behind with her sister wives. Her husband, Millford Bard Shipp, came to visit, impregnated her, and left. She still had medical school to complete.

Ellis taught my grandma midwifery, and my grandma never had kind words for Ellis's husband Millford because he was always making passes at various women. He was a creep who felt polygamy gave him license to act out and put his hands on whomever he pleased. Polygamy was not holy or inspired, in my opinion, but a practice created by men.

Great-great-grandfather was president of the church. He had six wives. There is a family reunion every year where everyone wears a name tag indicating which wife you are from. It turns my stomach about how excited these people get about this "polygamy celebration" every year. I refuse to go anymore. It's just weird how they all talk about it like it is the greatest thing ever.

My great-grandfather in Canada was a stake president, and years after the Manifesto he was instructed by Apostle John Taylor to get another wife. He did marry a woman from Utah and from then on spent half of the year in Canada and half in Utah with his new family. He then had children who were the same ages as his grandchildren. My grandma (his daughter) said many, many times to me that her mother was never the same after her husband took a second wife, that it broke her mother's heart. I abhor polygamy.

My ancestor's family practiced polygamy by official Church sanction well into the period after the 1890 manifesto that supposedly ended it. The multiple wives were kept as different families under different names to hide their secrets. This institutionally initiated lying created dysfunctional, divided homes with "secrets" (such as child abuse) under the cover of full church activity and faithfulness. My grandfather, a child of a polygamous home, was a bishop while being an alcoholic. Two of his children committed suicide. Yet it was all buried because he had grown up with an appreciation for "secrets."

My mother's life was one of massive depression. I read her journals and saw that the pain and agony of growing up in the wake of polygamy under false pretenses was horrible and ugly. This could not have been the work of any God.

I recently watched, together with my adult children and my wife, the story of the "lost boys" from Colorado City, Arizona, who have no hope of marrying because of polygamy. Many of my children didn't realize that this same situation had occurred while polygamy was practiced among "real" Mormons. I related the sad story of Bishop Warren Snow and the young man he ordered to be castrated in order for Snow to have a certain young bride for himself. They almost didn't believe it; my wife took several hours to comprehend it. Many active Mormons avoid thinking about all the harm and pain that polygamy created.

My grandmother related to me the sadness expressed to her by her father who never knew his own father because he had too many wives. Sadness was obvious in the lost boys and stolen lives and loneliness of young women. But the sadness was compounded when my great-grandfather was excommunicated because he thought the 1890 Manifesto wasn't real and thought that he was supposed to go on hiding and practicing polygamy, as that's what he had been told to do for years. He died as sad as could be upon finally realizing that the church abandoned him for practicing polygamy, a principle they had promised would *never, ever* end.

Polygamy was a man-made error, just like many other incorrect doctrines. And the LDS Church must somehow come up with an institutional apology for some of these errors. I think the church's survival depends on it. The little, hidden Gospel Topics essay on the church's website on polygamy defends it and doesn't even begin to address the wrongness of it.

Sorry, college professor giving a midterm. Finished the survey but don't have time to write what I want to here. Short version: child and grand-child of polygamists, but I am "Free at last, free at last!"

As a person with ancestors who were polygamists, I felt a sense of pride knowing that these ancestors had lived the "higher law." Learning that an ancestor had married a fifteen year old (his fourth wife) while serving as a mission president in Denmark in the mid-1800s and that she gave birth in Utah at sixteen years of age shortly after arriving with him after his mission ended (but before they could be "sealed" in a temple)—all this pretty much changed my mind.

It seems now that polygamy was more a reward for men who were "faithful priesthood holders" and that the "rules" around polygamy were only followed when convenient and all sorts of exceptions were made. It no longer feels like a "higher law" to me!

Emma Hale Smith and the Prophet Joseph Smith

James and Mary Oakey and family (Sarah, my grandmother, standing)

Seven of Brigham Young's wives; back row (left to right): Naamah Carter Young, Lucy B. Young, Amelia Folsom Young; front row (left to right): Margaret Pierce Young, Zina D. H. Young, Emily Dow Partridge Young, Harriet Barney Young

Brigham Young, second president of the LDS Church and husband to 55 wives

"What," says one, "do you mean we should understand that Deity consists of man and woman?" Most certainly I do. If I believe anything that God has ever said about himself, and anything pertaining to the creation and organization of man upon the earth, I must believe that Deity consists of man and woman.... There never was a God, and there never will be in all eternities, except they are made of these two component parts; a man and a woman; the male and the female.

—Erastus Snow, nineteenth-century LDS apostle

-8-

Our Mothers Who Art in Heaven

I BEGAN THIS morning with my usual ritual. I sit in the rose-colored chair in my quiet bedroom and breathe for a few moments. In my mind I see a larger-than-life, ageless, shimmering, impressionistic as if in watercolors, Divine Couple. He is to my left, She is to my right. Behind me are heavenly hosts, sometimes my ancestors, a few dear ones no longer on this earth, and all interested angels. (I don't mean to be greedy, but the holographic nature of heaven means that each of us can have it all, all the time.) I speak softly a little verse I wrote many years ago:

> Spirit hands are on my head
> Father, Mother blessing me.
> Comfort courses down like rain
> Cleansing and caressing me.

Light and warmth move through my head, my neck, my chest, my torso, legs, feet. I meditate for a while, using the mantra I claimed many years ago. "Shalom...shalom...shalom..." The meaning and the feeling are welcome: "Peace...." I speak my gratitudes, and then we do our blessings. I speak the words, and Father and Mother and I together send out peace and love and well-being and inspiration to everyone on my personal list, and then we cover the planet with grace. Then I request a blessing for myself, for my day, for my work, for guidance, and that into my day will come whoever I might need and whoever might need me.

AN ICON THAT permeates much of Utah and Mormon culture is the beehive. The idea of "Deseret," a word in the Book of Mormon interpreted as "honey bee," found its way as a beehive onto the "Flag of the Kingdom of God of the State of Deseret" and is the official state emblem of Utah today. Interestingly, the beehive is also a strong symbol in Freemasonry, and in some of the literature has been associated with the ancient goddess. We Mormons pride ourselves on being very much like the beehive in our industry and communal cooperation. We do not pause to reflect on the fact that, unlike the matriarchal beehive, our community manages without its Queen.

A little girl once wrote a letter: "Dear God, are boys really better than girls? I know you are one, but try to be fair." Once you stop to think about it, the idea that the earth and all its inhabitants were created by a male (even an omnipotent God Male) is, at best, irrational. All of us—you, me, the deer in the forest, the elephant on the tundra, the honeybee, the lily, the peacock—all were thoughts that became things over billions of years directed by the two that are One: MotherGoddessFatherGod. But over the centuries the children were careless and the divine word was broken. Parts were lost until all that was left of the word was FatherGod. That broken word feels like a broken home. I know this sounds more like poetry than theology, but sometimes I trust poetry more than I trust theology.

Still, MotherGoddess could never be entirely lost. The Prophet Joseph Smith and many others throughout the ages remembered her. In 1839, Joseph taught the doctrine to the same Zina Diantha Huntington who became one of his wives. Zina had lost her mother and was deep in grief. Joseph told her that she would surely see her mother again on the other side, but that something even more amazing was in store. Zina was told, "You will meet and become acquainted with your eternal Mother, the wife of your Father in Heaven. How could there be a Father without a Mother? How could a Father claim his title unless there were also a Mother to share that parenthood?" Eliza Roxcy Snow, another wife of the Prophet, was given the same teaching, and she memorialized it in a poem that became a hymn, sung by congregations today as one of the most loved in the Mormon hymnal.

Back in the 70s when I lived in Provo, Utah, Aunt Mamie told me that up on the old family property in Dingle, Idaho, in a very old cabin that had been a storage shed for a long time there were boxes and boxes of old magazines and papers. I couldn't bear the thought of mice and mildew destroying possible treasures, so I scooped up Aunt Mamie and we drove to Dingle. From the dust and cobwebs (and yes, the mice) I pulled out and boxed up a couple hundred copies of very old periodicals that had precious names of ancestor owners on the covers. Mary Oakey—that gutsy great-grandmother who had said no to polygamy—had a few years later held and read by coal oil lamps many of these papers and written at the top her name with the same hands that had helped to make a dugout to sleep in and a homestead to farm. I would share these papers with cousins. But when I picked up a slim book published in 1856 in Liverpool, I said, "Aunt Mamie, I think this one is for me." It was the first volume of poems by Eliza R. Snow.

"Of course," she said. "It is for you."

I opened the book to the first poem, the words to the hymn we sing as "O My Father." Eliza had titled it differently, for she had written it as a prayer to the Divine Parents:

INVOCATION,
or the
ETERNAL FATHER AND MOTHER

This poem had been the first tiny window that ever opened for me in the solid structure of patriarchy, showing a heaven that is home to the divine feminine. The last three verses are:

In the heav'ns are parents single?
No: the thought makes reason stare!
Truth is reason; truth eternal
Tells me I've a mother there.

When I leave this frail existence—
When I lay this mortal by
Father, Mother, may I meet you
In your royal courts on high?

Then at length, when I've completed
All you sent me forth to do,
With your mutual approbation
Let me come and dwell with you.

For decades now, as I have sat in Mormon congregations and sung this hymn and heard occasional references to deity as both Mother and Father, I have experienced it as a promised gift that is not yet given. *Somewhere—I've a Mother there.* Here the house is full of Father and empty of Mother. On the mantle is a double picture frame with the image of Father in one half and a blank space in the other. I see in my diary that thirty-five years ago I was writing how it felt to live in a Motherless House, the spiritual home that is my patriarchal world, my patriarchal church.

I live in a Motherless house
A broken home.
How it happened I cannot learn.

When I had words enough to ask
"Where is my Mother?"
No one seemed to know
And no one thought it strange
That no one else knew either.

I live in a Motherless house.
They are good to me here
But I find that no kindly
Patriarchal care eases the pain.

I yearn for the day
Someone will look at me and say
"You certainly do look like your Mother."

I walk the rooms
Search the closets
Look for something that might
Have belonged to her—
A letter, a dress, a chair.
Would she not have left a note?

I close my eyes
And work to bring back her touch, her face.
Surely there must have been
A Motherly embrace
I can call back for comfort.
I live in a Motherless house,
Motherless and without a trace.

Who could have done this?
Who would tear an unweaned infant
From its Mother's arms
And clear the place of every souvenir?

I live in a Motherless house.
I lie awake and listen always for the word
That never comes, but might.
I bury my face
In something soft as a breast.

I am a child—
Crying for my Mother in the night.

I WAS HUNGRY, and I was angry. Who stole our Mother? How did we lose our memory of the female in the divine, which affects our memory of the divine in the female? How did we allow something to happen that is so breathtakingly injurious to the whole family?

I remember the day in the late 70s after our family had moved from Utah to Northern California, when my husband Gerald excitedly ran in from a day in San Francisco with a book in his hand, saying, "Blossom, I saw this in the window of a bookstore and I knew you had to have it!" *When God was a Woman* by Merlin Stone. As I devoured the book I wrote in my diary of becoming "angry, excited, joyful." Little notes were passed to me from history, mementoes of my Mother. Windows opened and light entered a dark space. And then I learned windows were opening all over the world. Something large was happening! The books started coming so fast I could not read them all. The titles tell the story, and these are just the few that are within arm's reach on my bookshelf. *The Goddess Re-Awakening...A God Who Looks Like Me...The Feminine Face of God...The Divine Feminine: the Biblical Imagery of God as Female...The Return of the Mother...The Feminine Dimension of the Divine...The Great Cosmic Mother...In All Her Names...The Once and Future Goddess....*

What I had read somewhere was true—"The farther back you push the history of man, the larger looms the figure of woman." Both mortal and divine. I recalled standing in the Jerusalem museum as the museum director pointed out certain artifacts as showing the transition from worship of the female to worship of the male. I had been dumbfounded—MotherGoddess under glass.

Back in 1983 I clipped out an article from the LDS *Church News* with the headline, "Scholars expose a 'cover-up'":

> A cover-up was exposed at BYU's J. Rueben Clark Law School recently.... [S]everal speakers at the 32nd Annual Symposium on the Archaeology of the Scriptures...pointed accusing fingers back through time [at those] responsible for "covering up" valuable information about ancient Hebrew goddess worship...

in ancient homes [as well as in] the temple…for 236 of the 370 years prior to the destruction of the temple in 586 B.C.

But what had been lost was being found! And I was one of the beneficiaries. As I immersed myself in these riches, I felt as if I had reached out and caught a spark of God. That godly impulse was vibrating within me and demanding that I do something. But what? One day as I was hiking the hills above my home, thinking of all the women from all the ages who had owned, lost, or found the feminine divine, it fell into place. I would just let them speak. It would be a play, and each of these women could tell her story. And so was born my one-woman play, *Mother Wove the Morning*, in which I play sixteen women throughout history in search of God the Mother.

More than three hundred times I performed this play, traveling scene by scene from the Paleolithic, where humans knew only the goddess, the moon, the woman who bleeds and opens to bear a child—through the shadowy history of goddesses being superseded by gods—Rachel in the Bible sitting on her precious stolen teraphim, mementoes of the ancient order in which the mothers were honored and the goddess remembered—a woman in Greece, hearing in the theatre the new and unlikely story that Athena sprang from the forehead of Zeus and that the father is the only true parent of the child—a priestess in Egypt assured by a priest that men are nearer the form of the divine than are women, just as Ptah existed prior to Isis who had always been the oldest of the old—a witch in chains waiting to be burned in the Middle Ages for being a healer and a wise woman in service to the goddess.

There were also the sunnier stories, bright memories shared by a Gnostic woman that Jesus spoke of his Mother, the Holy Spirit—by a Native American honoring Thinking Woman, who thought the turquoise and thought the rabbit and the fish and you and me—by a Shaker, who recalls what all the Mamas sang clear back to Africa, about that "great shining black Mother of us all"—by a Jewish woman waiting for the Shekinah of the

Sabbath, the feminine part of God. And by Emma Smith, who rejoices in Joseph's teaching of a Mother in Heaven, but concludes in sorrow and confusion that if what her husband teaches is true, then the Father "must have many wives, more even than Joseph!"

AND THERE IT IS. The unique awfulness that we Mormons have to deal with in our efforts to invite our Mother back into the family. In nineteenth-century Utah, an unfortunate marriage took place. Brigham Young officiated, aided by many of the presiding brethren. Brother Joseph's teaching about a Heavenly Mother and his teaching about polygamy were wed in eternal marriage, and that strange union has never been dissolved. The result is that the Ghost has another vital field of Mormon experience to haunt—the whole of heaven, one Father surrounded by his wives, our many Mothers in Heaven.

In early Utah, Apostle Orson Pratt, who was frequently used by Brigham Young to articulate doctrine, said, regarding the multitudes of spirit children begotten by the Father:

> If the Father of these spirits…had secured to himself, through the everlasting covenant of marriage, many wives, as the prophet David did in our world, the period required to people a world would be shorter, within certain limits, in proportion to the number of wives. For instance, if it required one hundred thousand million of years to people a world like this, as above stated, it is evident that, with a hundred wives, this period would be reduced to only one thousand million of years. Therefore, a Father, with these facilities, could increase his kingdoms with his own children, in a hundred fold ratio above that of another who had only secured to himself one wife.

Apostle John Taylor, who later became president of the church, said:

> Knowest thou not that eternities ago thy spirit, pure and holy, dwelt in the Heavenly Father's bosom, and in his presence, and with thy mother, one of the Queens of heaven, surrounded by the brother and sister spirits in the spirit world, among the Gods?

It was also proposed by a number of Mormon leaders in the nineteenth century that Jesus Christ himself was a polygamist. On one occasion Brigham Young said:

> The Scripture says that He, the Lord, came walking in the Temple, with His train; I do not know who they were, unless His wives and children.

Recently the official LDS Church has explained the doctrine of eternal progression more as "becoming godly" than "becoming gods." We have already seen that today's church authorities would not endorse all the ideas put forth by Brigham Young and other leaders who spoke with his approval, but the teachings regarding a multiplicity of Heavenly Mothers are still widespread in Mormondom and become food for the Ghost of Eternal Polygamy. I recall clearly a conversation with a BYU professor I respected. When I asked his observations on the idea of our Heavenly Mother, he answered with a smile, "Well, all I know is—She *are!*" Only a few months ago in my own congregation, a friend reported a conversation in priesthood meeting in which a man I know said, "Don't you think that the reason we know hardly anything about Heavenly Mother is just that…well, there are so *many* of them!" And recently the *Salt Lake Tribune* printed among the comments in response to a beautiful textile-based artwork at BYU dealing with Mother in Heaven: "Since multiple wives are required in the first-class section of the Celestial kingdom, shouldn't the term be Heavenly Mothers?"

I HAVE NOTICED a growing impulse in the Mormon community to speak more of our divine Mother, generally just in using the words, "Our Heavenly Parents," or "Our Father and Mother in Heaven." But sometimes more. This summer, the young and wonderfully enthusiastic bishop of my ward gave an inspiring talk to the Young Women one evening up in the mountains at Girl's Camp, focusing on our Heavenly Mother, the qualities she must have, and asking the girls to observe qualities in themselves that surely came from their divine Mother. And not long ago our Relief Society president gave a talk in sacrament meeting entitled, "Mother in Heaven—Our Need to Know." She expressed that sometimes information is given out on a "Need to Know" basis, and that surely for us as women, "There is a *need*, a need to *know* our Heavenly Mother because she is from whence we came." That need, sabotaged by plural marriage, was stated profoundly by Sarah Bringhurst Familia, who sent to me a piece she had written for one of the popular Mormon blogs, "Times and Seasons," showing that "the old adage about us all being children of the same God turns out to be only half true." I share here an excerpt from that blog post:

> Eternal polygamy turns my Heavenly Mother into a sort of amorphous crowd, indistinct, unknowable, fading into obscurity.
>
> When I try to imagine a heaven with one reigning Patriarch surrounded by many wives, my mind and soul descend into darkness, doubt and confusion. Trying to reconcile the idea of eternal polygamy, which deeply offends my heart and spirit, with my belief in a loving Heavenly Father has been a struggle for me during much of my life, and at times has distanced me from Him and from my husband and left me feeling depressed, worthless, and angry. That's a scary, dark place to be.
>
> Ultimately, I realized that either my belief in God or my belief in polygamy had to go. They were mutually incompatible. I was not capable of believing in the God of polygamy because He was no god I would ever want to worship. For me, the divine picture only comes into focus when I [know] the glorious reality of one Heavenly Mother who embodies every power and perfection in Her female form, and stands side-by-side with my Heavenly Father in wisdom, love, authority, and counsel.
>
> President David O. McKay often quoted this statement by Rev. Theodore Hesburgh: "The most important thing a father can do for his children is to love their mother." No amount of telling me that "Heavenly Father loves His daughters just as much as He loves His sons" rings true to me, until I feel for myself the way He loves my Mother. My assurance of the love my Heavenly Parents have for me and my trust in their plan

of happiness flow directly from my understanding of the even
deeper love and partnership they share with one another.

Many Mormon women, and sometimes men, take to the Internet to ask the questions and express the pain about our Motherless House and propose some timid (or sometimes bold) answers: "I
think we're going to find that our Heavenly Mother is simply half of
what we've been calling our Heavenly Father all this time." "It seems
to me that the Holy Ghost must be female, maybe what we've been
calling our Mother. If you trace the imagery back and back the Holy
Spirit takes us to Wisdom, which is female, and to Sophia...."

And we try to make sense of the declarations we hear that every family needs a father and a mother—certainly not two dads—
as we look at our own spiritual family and see there not just two
dads but three—the Father, the Son, and the Holy Ghost, and not
a Mother in sight. It is my belief that when we, in our small Mormon corner of God's universe, are able truly to expel the Ghost of
Eternal Polygamy, we will "shout aloud and sing for joy" and know
that one huge obstacle has been shattered and melts away. We can
think a healed thought and speak a healed word, speak of and to the
two who are One, our MotherGoddessFatherGod. The hopeful but
misty thought that "I've a Mother there" will give way to the experience that "I've a Mother *here*." We will know Him, Her, Them, Us,
the Divine Family unbroken, bringing part to whole and whole to
part, singing the indispensable She who had been forgotten but is
now found, singing the wholeness, singing the holiness.

How URGENT IS the need to reclaim God the Mother? Three men
that I respect give their answers.

Anthropologist Raphael Patai:

> The God of Judaism is undoubtedly a father-symbol...nor can
> there be any doubt as to the need answered by this image....
> However, there is an equally great, or possibly even greater need
> for yet another symbol: that of the divine woman who appears

in many different forms throughout the world yet remains basically the same everywhere.

Mythologist Robert Graves:

The more than usually miserable state of the world demands that the supreme Godhead be redefined, that the repressed desire of the Western races for some practical form of goddess worship be satisfied.

Religious scholar Andrew Harvey:

At the end of his life, the great Indian mystic Aurobindo...said, "If there is to be a future, it will wear the crown of feminine design." ...Everything, I believe, now depends on how the human race imagines and relates to the sacred feminine and the Mother.... The Mother, as always, continues to extend to all beings complete grace and complete help.

We are part of the process, the discovery, the welcome home. Here is what I believe and what I have experienced. If I dare to accept the radical promise of Jesus in the gospel of Luke that "the kingdom of God is within you," unlikely ground as that might seem, it holds marvelous disclosures. Treasures from the kingdom's treasury are found outside in the world, in chapels and temples and libraries and the skies and the rocks and other people's eyes. But that is not where the kingdom is found. I close my eyes, open my heart, and turn on the light. And there—just like a surprise party!—all the smiling royalty—one court, one King, one Queen.

I am a castle. The Kingdom and Queendom of God is within.

Other Voices:

"I long for a heaven not darkened by the shadows of polygamy"

For me personally, the doctrine of polygamy reduces me as a woman to nothing more than breeding stock, little more than an animal. It raises the deepest fears of my heart about why we don't know more about Heavenly Mother, and means that our doctrine of "heavenly parents" is nothing more than lip service.

It has also brought on a crisis of faith about whether I want to continue to be a member of this church. I have seen this tear apart marriages and families because women cannot live with it, their husbands cannot give them any comfort or explanation, and the church continues not to clarify. I just do my best not to think about it.

In conjunction with the taboos about speaking about/to Heavenly Mother and rumors that there are perhaps many heavenly mothers, the prospect of eternal polygamy makes me wonder if the celestial kingdom is a heaven for women or a hell. In all honesty, I would rather be an angel with good, honest work to do, rather than being in the celestial kingdom, silent, polygamous, and eternally pregnant. I long for a simpler Christian view of heaven not darkened by the shadows of polygamy.

In this last year, I had a friend and lifelong member of the church leave with her whole family because of her understanding of polygamy. She said that she asked questions of everyone she could find and no one could ever answer her. She said, "Emma's injustice alone is reason enough to leave the church."

I don't know if polygamy is the highest form of marriage. I don't know if we don't know much about our Heavenly Mother because we have many of them. I have said that if heaven is polygamy then I'd rather not go. When I ponder these things I feel awful and angry and disconnected from God.

I have spent the last few years pouring over the scriptures about polygamy—I've read Doctrine and Covenants Section 132 a million times—and I've prayed about it until my voice was hoarse and I've had no tears left. I've spoken to bishops, institute teachers, family, friends, teachers—anyone who will listen—and have gotten nothing more than a lot of "I don't knows."

Honestly, I prefer the "I don't knows" to speculations about how many wives God has and which of our Heavenly Mothers we descend from.

From finding out about polygamy as a young girl to later learning about God's many wives (of all races and cultures) in an after-class discussion with my BYU Book of Mormon professor whom I adored, the idea of eternal polygamy has always been very upsetting to me.

Although I have chosen to reject this aspect of Mormon doctrine, I have witnessed how this has been a source of extreme stress, sadness, and loneliness for individuals and families in the Church.

Upon learning of polygamy as a teenage girl, I felt confusion and fear. I felt like God did not love me or value me as much as he did his sons. I felt like my importance and significance was reduced to what I gave to a man, and nothing more. I struggled for many years to accept this doctrine, hearing so many excuses, but none that helped. My sister concluded that the reason we don't speak of Heavenly Mother is because there is more than one.

I can only assume that my eternal future, as defined by the LDS Church, is to be a nameless, voiceless mother whose only job is to be one of many, one who produces offspring and is cut off from her children so they do not defile her name as they do God's. I think this doctrine is emotionally abusive. It tortures many women. It is not of God. It is of man. I ache for the thousands upon thousands of women who have suffered and still suffer under this doctrine.

But worst of all were the whispers that God approved polygamy because that's how *he* lived. In fact, sometimes they were much more than whispers. During a discussion about Mary and the conception of Jesus, one of my Mission Training Center teachers stated baldly, "Well, we *know* that God is a polygamist. And evidently Mary was one of his wives."

My mother believed that "reconciling ourselves" to the doctrine of polygamy was essential for salvation. I heard many things in church that supported this idea and it worried me greatly, from about age twelve onward. She often joked with like-minded friends that they must have "come from the same mother in heaven."

I was taught that because men preside over women, women only become goddesses under their husband's and father's rule. They don't own their divinity. This was supposedly why we never hear about Heavenly Mother—because (1) she was one of many, and (2) she was only a demigod, having power only through her husband. I was taught that polygamy was in place because it would help men progress and if women refused, they would be punished.

I don't believe any of that now. I do not believe in a cruel, misogynist God. The God I believe in considers me equal in every way to my husband. The current LDS culture doesn't teach about a Mother Goddess and Father God of equality.

I reject the notion that Heavenly Mother doesn't deserve recognition, that she is to be hidden because she is lesser or delicate. She is a Goddess, after all. I think if we sought her as much as we seek Father, our gospel understanding would be complete. We are foolish to think we can learn about a heavenly family and champion the traditional family model while operating in a Single Father God household.

Do we have multiple "Mothers in Heaven?" Is Heavenly Father a polygamist? Will my wife (my one wife) devote herself eternally to bearing spirit children? Right now, both of us would rather she spend eternity composing great music.

A successful marriage requires falling in love many times, always
with the same person.

—Mignon McLaughlin

-9-
"How Do I Love Thee?"

URING THE SAME years in the early 1840s that the Prophet
Joseph was taking to himself in marriage more than thirty
women in his city by the Mississippi, across the Atlantic
in her home on Wimpole Street in London, Elizabeth Barrett
Browning was writing poetry. The poem that is the most famous, the
poem that college girls like me memorized and recited to ourselves
for the beauty of its words and for its vision of eternal love, is #43
from *Sonnets to the Portuguese*.

> How do I love thee? Let me count the ways.
> I love thee to the depth and breadth and height
> My soul can reach, when feeling out of sight
> For the ends of being and ideal grace.
> I love thee to the level of every day's
> Most quiet need, by sun and candle-light.
> I love thee freely, as men strive for right;
> I love thee purely, as they turn from praise.
> I love thee with the passion put to use
> In my old griefs, and with my childhood's faith.
> I love thee with a love I seemed to lose
> With my lost saints. I love thee with the breath,
> Smiles, tears, of all my life; and, if God choose,
> I shall but love thee better after death.

MANY OF THE women who arrived in Nauvoo brought with them a few precious books. I'm imagining now that I see atop a small rough-hewn table an embroidered doily, and atop that, a book. The title is *Pride and Prejudice*, the very fashionable novel by Jane Austen, that Englishwoman. The hand of the woman who placed it there, with a bookmark halfway through, belongs to Helen—or perhaps Sarah—or perhaps Emily or Lucy or a number of other women. The reading has been interrupted with an important message from a brother, father, or friend. "The Prophet Joseph wishes to have a private interview with you."

When the book again is picked up, perhaps the following day, the reader can hardly discern the words on the page. They keep bumping into words circling through her mind that she will never be able to forget, words spoken with great seriousness by the man she reveres as her prophet, words that are some variation of the following: "I have a message for you. I have been commanded of God to take another wife, and you are the woman." Helen—or perhaps Sarah—or perhaps Emily or Lucy or a number of other women—closes the book and places it back on the doily on the little rough-hewn table, perhaps not to be opened again. Fiction has been overpowered by the strangest of facts. Elizabeth Bennet will win the love prize. (Our woman has read this book before.) Mr. Darcy will devote his life to making her happy, and the two of them will be pronounced man and wife, unique in each other's eyes and always first in each other's heart. The woman at the table stares out the window and sees nothing, not even the cypress tree whose needles are beginning their seasonal shed. God has spoken and her life will never be the same.

I BELIEVE IN romantic love. I have such respect, even awe for this altered state of consciousness—at its worst a kind of insanity, at its best a kind of godliness. Most everyone yearns for it. In spite of failure, broken heart, broken dream, pain that makes you hold yourself and weep, you taste the yearning and you fall for it, fall for falling in love.

History tells me that the idea of taking romantic love seriously developed like democracy did, springing from the radical notion of the importance of the individual. The thought that romantic love and actual marriage should exchange rings to form a new union!—that is as revolutionary as America is, the full flower of liberty opening of its own, all voluntary, hands freely raised because *I will* and *I must* and *I stand responsible* for this great act, this grand frontier adventure where *I* choose, where there is not master and slave or buyer and bought, where both are created equal and equally invest and equally commit and pledge allegiance to each other, loving by consent of the lovers. I salute the flag of wedded lovers, I do, as they dare the most magnificent pursuit of happiness.

It's so messy. It's so irresistible. When you're caught in the very best wave—delight and passion and wonder and respect and desire and admiration and devotion—it feels like...like God has spoken and you know your life will never be the same. *Like God has spoken directly to you!* Love has created of an ordinary room a private cathedral where two can meet to worship God in each other.

Joseph's polygamy had little to do with romantic love. It came by commandment that no one seemed entirely to understand. Joseph wedded families together in his eternal kingdom by wedding women to him. It created alliances like the royals did when they married off a daughter or a sister to secure land or strengthen the power of the crown. The promise made to Helen—or perhaps Sarah—or perhaps Emily or Lucy or a number of other women—was that this union would open doors to heavenly riches that were available in no other way, securing for her in heaven the highest position available, and perhaps even more importantly securing that blessing for her entire family. Church Historian Leonard Arrington wrote in his diary:

> There was a very definite feeling that persons could not achieve exaltation without linkages to persons who were essentially

assured of exaltation. [It was believed that Joseph Smith] was certain to be a king, a ruler over many, a head of a dispensation in the next life.

Lucy Walker later wrote regarding her feelings at Joseph's proposal, "[I was] called to place myself upon the altar a living sacrifice, perhaps to brook the world in disgrace…all my dreams of happiness blown to the four winds." Later, after what she described as a remarkable spiritual affirmation, Lucy wrote of polygamy as a "source of comfort," and said, "We accepted it to obey a command of God." Helen Mar Kimball, who was still fourteen when she married the Prophet and was fifteen when she became a widow, spent much of her life in serious depression, yearning for a life she could not live. Later she wrote that Joseph's proposal, which she found "repugnant,"

> had a similar effect to a sudden shock of a small earthquake…. My father had but one Ewe Lamb, but willingly laid her upon the alter: how cruel this seamed to the mother whose heartstrings were already stretched until they were ready to snap asunder….

Earlier Joseph had insisted that Helen's father Heber "surrender his wife, his beloved Vilate, and give her to Joseph in marriage." After some days of deepest anguish by Heber and by Vilate, the offering was made. Joseph rejoiced at Heber's devotion to him and told Heber it was merely a test. Yes, God spared Abraham the sacrifice—God spared Heber the sacrifice—but God did not spare Lucy and Helen and thousands of other Mormon women the fully enacted sacrifice of placing themselves on the altar as directed by their prophet.

There were women who said no to Joseph and suffered no repercussions, but for many who said yes, the story was about the same: give up earthly happiness in love and marriage in exchange for the matchless blessing of being intimately connected to God's prophet and therefore intimately connected to God.

In Utah, polygamy was also seen as business, the earthly business of reproduction to fill the territory with children sired by worthy men, but primarily the godly business of creating family kingdoms bound for heaven. Romance was not the goal. Brigham said regarding a man's wives, "Never love them so but that you can leave them at a moment's warning without shedding a tear." Another time he made the oft-quoted quip that "when his wives got tired he could take them home and change them for fresh ones." Brigham may have chuckled as he said those words, but I do not smile to report them, nor do I believe the women smiled in pioneer Utah to hear them or to experience Brigham's indifference. There is something in a woman that needs to feel loved, feel distinctive and extraordinary, feel wanted for the warmth of her own heart or the cleverness of her own mind, or perhaps the color of her eyes or hair or the sound of her voice or the way she moves her hands—something delightful that makes the man suddenly notice that he's humming, makes him wake in the morning to the thought of her, hungry to be in her presence for her presence is home. These are the things that a woman would like to believe pushes the man to ask her to be his wife, not the fact that he comes by command of God. She needs to feel neither first nor subsequent but singular.

It was not possible to drive these desires from Mormon polygamous wives, no matter how deeply they felt Joseph and Brigham were divinely inspired. Emmeline B. Wells, prominent writer and editor and seventh wife of Daniel H. Wells, defended plural marriage in public, but poured her sorrow out in her journals. These words are from 1874, one year after Mary Oakey left her husband James:

> O, if my husband could only love me even a little and not seem to be perfectly indifferent to any sensation of that kind. He cannot know the cravings of my nature; he is surrounded with love on every side, and I am cast out.... How much sorrow I have known in place of the joy I looked forward to.

A favorite book on my shelf is *The Psychology of Romantic Love* by Dr. Nathaniel Branden. He writes:

> Romantic love is not a fantasy or an aberration but one of the great possibilities of our existence, one of the great adventures, and one of the great challenges. I am writing from the conviction that ecstasy is one of the normal factors of our emotional life, or can be.... Romantic love is a *passionate spiritual-emotional-sexual attachment...that reflects a high regard for the value of each other's person*.... Romantic love is not a myth, waiting to be discarded, but, for most of us, a discovery, waiting to be born...the exquisite joy of one self encountering another.... In romantic love two selves are celebrated as they are celebrated in no other context.... Romantic love, in the context of an exclusive relationship, may in the end be the most exciting adventure there is.

Branden goes on to say that one of the conditions of romantic love "is equality—since the relationship of a superior to an inferior, or a master to a subordinate, cannot qualify as romantic love." Polygamous romantic love is an oxymoron for both man and woman. Polygamy does not increase a man's emotional opportunities—it halves them, or quarters them, or eighths them. No man has an endless supply of intimate giving. The beauty of romantic love is its depth, not its breadth. And for a woman polygamy is giving all and receiving part. To "adulterate" is to "render something poorer in quality by adding another substance, typically an inferior one, to make impure, degrade, spoil, taint." "Adulterate" and "adultery" are sister words, and in this sense polygamy functions precisely as adultery does, adding something that taints to something that was pure. There are those who argue that an "open marriage" or a "polyamorous arrangement" are superior configurations. I don't believe that. I see a non-monogamous marriage as the adulterating anti-miracle that turns wine into water.

One woman who responded to my survey wrote:

I met my husband when we were fourteen years old. He was the smartest boy, and had the most gentle, mischievous, green eyes. I felt so safe around him. I dated other men in college, but no one, no one held a candle to my sweetheart. He fills up all the empty places in my heart and always knows the right thing to say when I am down. I know that I can do that for him too, and it brings me indescribable joy. My husband is my best friend, my soul mate, the one person on this planet who knows me and appreciates and loves me anyway. He is my greatest source of happiness.

Despite this, there has always been a lingering pain in my heart that makes me hold back. There is always a piece of me that wonders... "If I die first, will he marry again and be sealed to another woman, making us eternal polygamists?"

That thought has made me cautious, wondering if there would be a place in the universe far enough away for me to hide if I were on the other side of the veil and my dear love was having another woman sealed to him forever. Practically speaking, this has had an impact on intimate aspects of our eternal love. As my marriage has grown closer over the past seven years, the pain of this issue has only worsened. Could God break my heart forever and call that heaven?

AN ANACHRONISM IS "a person or a thing that is chronologically out of place, especially one from a former age that is incongruous in the present." As if in Shakespeare's day Macbeth pulled a pocket watch out of his robe. Or as if the president of the United States today should call for his horse and buggy. Polygamy was an anachronism even in Kirtland and Nauvoo and certainly in Utah. It was lifted out of an ancient civilization where it was an accepted part of the culture and transplanted to a progressive Western nation that proved a totally inhospitable habitat. Here it stood out like a bleeding thumb, could not make a good home for itself, and finally collapsed.

Collapsed but strangely still breathes. Today, nearly two centuries after Joseph's original introduction of plural marriage, the phenomenon—now with even more layers of anachronism—lives on. Lisa—or Karen—or Skylar or Hailey—or one of a number of other contemporary Mormon women—who lives on the avenues in Salt

Lake City, or in Phoenix or Toronto or London—comes home from the gym, or from the office, or from picking up the kids at school. Husband will be home late. Supper. Kids in bed. She showers, gets into her favorite nightie, looks through her DVDs for something light and romantic to entertain her until her man arrives. *Sleepless in Seattle—When Harry Met Sally—An Affair to Remember*—or maybe, yes, *Pride and Prejudice*—that great 2005 version with the final scene that is so delicious you have to rewind it at least once and you mouth the words as you hug your pillow. Nighttime, with the magnificent estate of Pemberley in the background. Newlyweds sit before each other, knees touching.

Mr. Darcy asks, "How are you this evening, my dear?"

Lizzy responds, "Very well...although I wish you would not call me 'my dear.'"

Darcy chuckles. "Why?"

"Because it's what my father always calls my mother when he's cross about something."

"What endearments am I allowed?"

"Well, let me think. 'Lizzy' for every day, 'My Pearl' for Sundays, and...'Goddess Divine'...but only on *very* special occasions."

"And...what should I call you when I am cross? 'Mrs. Darcy'?"

"No! No." Lizzy smiles. "You may only call me 'Mrs. Darcy' when you are completely, and perfectly, and incandescently happy."

"Then how are you this evening...Mrs. Darcy?" He kisses her forehead. "Mrs. Darcy." Her right cheek. "Mrs. Darcy." Her nose. "Mrs. Darcy." Her left cheek. "Mrs. Darcy." Finally kisses her tenderly on the mouth. "Mrs. Darcy."

Slow fade to black.

Be still, my heart.

And you know the best thing about this scene? All those plural "Mrs. Darcys" are only Lizzy.

THEN LISA—OR Karen—or Skylar or Hailey—or one of a number of other contemporary Mormon women—hears her husband come in. She sighs, and leans back into the pillows with a smile.

Or maybe with a smile that is a little wistful, even a little apprehensive. If she is one of the many, many Mormon women in whose home the sad and scary Ghost has taken up residence, she may move into that dim, familiar territory where God has played his terrible trick, that place where she is afraid that for her, sometime in the timeless, there may well be another Mrs. Darcy…and perhaps another…and another…. From a response to the survey:

> I ended up marrying a man who was a recent convert. One thing I liked about him was that he was appalled by the idea of polygamy. Finally! An actual male who felt the same as I did.
>
> But still, after we were married—polygamy moved in with us. Every time I would show affection to my husband, I immediately flashed to what the celestial kingdom was going to be like, and I saw that this man who I loved more than anything was basically going to be taken away from me and all these tender moments we had together would be shared with other women.
>
> I would cry inside, already feeling like part of me was living a polygamous relationship. I withheld love. I wasn't as kind as I wanted to be. I wasn't purposefully mean, but I was protecting myself. All this created a wedge between us. Polygamy was in our future, and I hated it!
>
> Luckily, all that changed one day when I began to read church history. The deeper I got into it, the more I knew it was all a big mistake. The Spirit confirmed it, and it felt so good! I could practically hear the Lord saying, "Noooo! Polygamy is wrong!"
>
> My marriage changed dramatically. I knew polygamy would never rear its head. My husband says I'm much kinder to him now, and we're both so grateful for the closeness we now feel.

Falling in love is a rich and hazardous event, and it deserves protection. It is a sort of trap whereby life snatches people by the twos—*only* by the twos—and ties them so tightly together that they can't get away until they learn something—learn about love, real love: being in, working in, living in, rising in, all begun by falling in. Two people falling in love.

Everyone deserves that priceless opportunity.

Other Voices:

"I've held back part of my heart"

When my husband told me one day, after many years of marriage, that he fully intended to be obedient to God in all things, including plural marriage, I felt a terrible rift being born between us. I asked him how we could be one as the Lord commands if he was desiring another woman, desiring her and her and her and her. How could this be heaven for me? He replied that I would be as happy as I would choose to be and that our children would soothe my loneliness. Plus, he added, God will make you like it. He wants you to be happy.

Since then the rift is ever there. A part of me is walled off, wondering how I can be with a man who looks forward to this future, knowing it pains me terribly, but feeling my suffering isn't his problem or concern. He has said only selfish and weak women reject polygamy because if God commands it, it is holy and pure.

Women have no power in our church, no voice and zero authority. No wonder there's so much depression among my Mormon sisters.

I found out my husband of thirty-two years was having an affair. He was never unfaithful up to that time, but he began studying doctrine and then made up his own mind that in heaven polygamy would be allowed. And if we weren't sealed to just one spouse after this life, why not live that way here? This thinking was part of the justification for his actions. We are putting our life and our marriage back together, outside the framework of the LDS Church.

Because my husband was still technically sealed to his first wife and was not allowed to have that sealing cancelled, there was a barrier created in my subconscious mind, one that remains today. The husband-wife relationship is clearly compromised when women have to share their husband, even as a possibility, even on paper. I love my husband dearly, but I have always unintentionally held back a part of my heart and soul because of the terrible thought that he is not fully mine. Now that our children are raised, I hope to focus more on us as a couple and see if I can find a way to heal this old deep-seated wound, a wound that should never have been there in the first place.

I know of at least five men who have been sealed to their current spouse in the temple, who have verbally expressed looking forward to having wives in the eternities, as they weren't fully happy with the wife they married and raised a family with.

One of these men actually was choosing his next-life plural wife, a girlfriend from high school that he did not marry because she was not LDS. He intended to have her temple work done when she died so he could have her sealed to him in the next life and be together with her forever.

He told his wife about this desire openly. It really hurt her, and it hurt me, too, to see how he was already happier knowing his wife wasn't the only one he was "stuck with." That conversation was almost as old as their marriage. Way to make your wife feel worthless!

I have been a bishop and have held other leadership positions, and I see the damage that Mormon polygamy still inflicts. Many are leaving the fold, and marriages are being destroyed.

Two immediate family members divorced at least partly because of errant LDS polygamy notions. One pursued anticipatory preparations with "futuristic" wives until his wife awoke to the nature of the pursuits and ended the marriage.

The other situation was a second marriage for both partners, but they were not sealed because the wife was sealed to her first husband who died early in an auto accident. Under common marital stresses she pursued divorce, repeatedly justifying the idea of divorce with such charges as: "You cannot be the father of our children in the next life anyway" (because the children are assumed to stay in the covenant of her sealing to her first husband).

I am disappointed that none of our church leaders have been willing to officially change the practice and policy to be in harmony with equality and agency. Sadly, we continue to give preferential privilege to men while perpetuating suffering upon women.

I am a marriage and family therapist who has worked for nearly twenty years primarily with LDS clients, and I can verify that polygamy continues to damage marriages. A man confided in me:

"My wife has told me that she plans to get remarried if I die first and seems to be open to the idea that might mean cancelling our sealing and spending eternity with someone else, even though I don't plan to remarry if she dies first. Ever since she told me this, I have kept my feelings in check. Outwardly we have a great marriage—twenty-eight years and four wonderful children. We're active in the church. But there is an intimate part of me that refuses to give our marriage 100% because I don't really know if we belong to each other or to potential others."

I have seen too much of the destructive implications the thought of eternal polygamy can bring to marriages, and I hope our church will take steps to end the pain and the confusion and help spouses live in the present moment and invest fully in each other.

When I got married, my bishop at the time wanted to meet with my husband and me. During the interview, he told me I better be careful to never upset my husband or my husband would choose a new wife in the eternities and I would be alone or have to live with this new wife forever.

Luckily, my husband doesn't buy into that or I wouldn't have married him. I told the bishop his comment was inappropriate, and he did apologize, but I have always wondered how many people he said that to and how it might have affected their marriages.

When my parents had been married for a little more than one year, my father told my mother that if he were asked to marry additional wives in heaven he would do so.

During the following year she grieved. She would often cry. When my father saw her tears, he would roll his eyes and walk away. With time, my mother lost her tender feelings for my father. He thought his way of thinking was righteous. My very faithful mother's heart was broken. This eventually led to divorce and heart-wrenching consequences for five children.

The idea of polygamy provided an entre—one of the shaping perspectives—for my wife becoming involved in an affair with a very active and believing Mormon man, after which she was excommunicated. Healing our marriage afterward was one factor of several that led us to disassociate from Mormonism. If polygamy wasn't a regular cultural current to modern Mormonism, things would likely have been different for us.

As a Mormon, I had grown up learning that polygamy could come back any time and would certainly meet us in the celestial kingdom. It hurt my stomach when I thought about it. It colored every crush I had, and carried through into my marriage. Knowing that you may have to watch your beloved also love another someday—even by commandment!—makes you hold back, just a little, so that something of you can be left when the blow comes.

When I was a believer, I prayed every day that my husband would die before I did so he couldn't be sealed to another woman and make me live in polygamy for eternity. What a way to conduct a marriage!

When I started dating my now-husband, I never dreamed that our first fight would be about polygamy in heaven. I told him I'm not doing that even if it means I'm cast into Outer Darkness. He was shocked. I don't blame him. I had just told him, the man I was going to marry, that I would sooner endure the torments of hell than endure polygamy with him.

I don't know what my husband thinks about polygamy almost five years after that conversation. I don't want to know. I do know that we are not stronger for the idea of polygamy. I know my parents are not stronger for it. We are strong *in spite of* it.

I married my first husband, "John," when I was twenty-one. We were sealed in the temple. A year and a half later he suddenly passed away in a motorcycle accident, leaving me eight months pregnant. A year after his passing, I became very close to John's best childhood friend, "Larry." We would date, but break up a lot primarily because he wanted a sealing for eternity, which I could not give him. It hurt.

Finally Larry and I married, saying we would figure out the sealing stuff later. As time passed, I told him I might be willing to break my first sealing.

We ended up with a surprise pregnancy at the beginning of our marriage. The pressure was really on me now to decide if I should attempt to break the sealing to John and be sealed to Larry. Which one should this child be paternally sealed to?

The stake president spoke with the office of the First Presidency and told us we should have the child born under the covenant of my first marriage just in case I had the baby early before I could be sealed to Larry, because a baby "born in the covenant" gets blessings and protections that children who are not "born in the covenant" do not receive.

Also, he said that they could break the baby's sealing to John and re-seal the baby to Larry after our own sealing covenant has been put in place.

But that sealing never happened because I couldn't bear breaking my sealing to John. It was always a touchy subject between Larry and me. He would tell me he needed to be sealed to his son and to his wife. I would stay up crying in my pillow, mourning John and feeling like I shouldn't have to divorce him on top of losing him, and also making it so he floats around unsealed and unexalted.

Larry and I are now going through a divorce. The sealing thing is a major part of this as we have never felt unified as other couples in the church do. This was the primary rift that destroyed our family.

Remember, all men would be tyrants if they could. If particular care and attention is not paid to the ladies we are determined to foment a rebellion, and will not hold ourselves bound by any laws in which we have no voice, or representation.

—Abigail Adams

I raise up my voice—not so I can shout, but so that those without a voice can be heard.... We cannot succeed when half of us are held back.

—Malala Yousafzai, Nobel Peace Laureate

-10-

Five Pennies Make a Nickel, and Women are the Pennies

I BEGIN THIS chapter on the Fourth of July. The flag is up on the front porch and later I will go down to the kitchen and make a potato salad and have some family fun. But writing this book is more than fun, it is my joy and my celebration and my contribution to liberty, justice, and equality. I want to spend some time now thinking about that word, "equality."

When I was recently in Nauvoo, Illinois, I walked along the "Trail of Hope," the road that led from the City of Joseph to the bank of the Mississippi River. The Mormons, 15,000 of them expelled from that state, walked this path with their families, their wagons and their animals, looking back at the temple they had sacrificed to complete and dedicate to the Lord all the while knowing they would leave it. Along that trail today are placards the LDS Church has placed, quotes from diaries and letters of those who left. One of the first quotes made me smile, an entry of June 7, 1846, from the diary of Louise Barnes Pratt:

> Last evening the ladies met to organize.... Several resolutions were adopted.... If the men wish to hold control over women, let them be on the alert. We believe in equal rights.

Interesting that we use the same word—"right"—to mean "correct" and also to mean "a moral or legal entitlement." In 1872 in Utah, when Mormon women published one of the first newspapers for women in the country, *Woman's Exponent*, they wrote large on the masthead, "The Rights of the Women of Zion and the Rights of Women of all Nations." And when they met as suffragists in homes, they sang their own words to the tune we Mormons know as "Hope of Israel":

Woman, Arise

Freedom's daughter, rouse from slumber,
See the curtains are withdrawn
Which so long thy mind hath shrouded
Lo! Thy day begins to dawn.

Woman, 'rise, thy penance o'er;
Sit thou in the dust no more.
Seize the scepter, hold the van,
Equal with thy brother, man!

"Equal" is another interesting word. We can use it to mean "the same as," or "of like quality or status." Typing that sentence I noticed that "quality" (a high level of value) just needs an "e" to become "equality." I like that. I don't want women and men to be "the same." But for women and men to see themselves and each other as "equal in quality"—that is something worth fighting for. My commitment on this Independence Day is to work on behalf of the woman who wrote to me:

As far as polygamy goes, it was just one more thing in the church that communicated to me that my value wasn't as high as a man's. Sort of like how you can exchange five pennies for one nickel—if we were money, you could exchange multiple women for one man. I never felt okay about it, and I was afraid that's how heaven would look.

Growing up I experienced so much sexism that my self-esteem, especially surrounding my gender, has always been low. Even to this day I struggle with feelings that men are better than me. That they know more. That the only way for me to be a legitimate human being is through being owned by one in marriage.

In 1980, Mormon scholar Dr. Hugh Nibley gave a talk entitled "Patriarchy and Matriarchy," in which he called both of those configurations "perversions," each having its own

> peculiar brand of corruption...men and women seeking power and gain at each other's expense.... So one must choose between patriarchy and matriarchy until the Zion of God is truly established upon the earth...that celestial order established in the beginning.

Likely there was never a general matriarchy to match the patriarchy that we have known for many centuries, but Dr. Riane Eisler, scholar, futurist and President of the Center for Partnership Studies, writes in *The Chalice and the Blade* about a number of ancient "remarkably equalitarian" societies where there was not "subordination and suppression" of either gender, particularly Crete where "for the last time in recorded history, a spirit of harmony between women and men as joyful and equal participants in life appears to pervade." Imagine!—a partnership society of women and men as joyful and equal participants.

That's the best word I know that can transcend "patriarchy" or "matriarchy"— "partnership." I could raise a flag to that kind of governing, in society, in family, in religion. And I would add to Dr. Nibley's observations on patriarchy and matriarchy that perhaps working toward partnership is one of the prerequisites to truly establishing "the Zion of God" upon the earth. Partnership doesn't mean "the same." The best business partners do not bring identical gifts to the table; they bring unique lights that when combined create a brightness that is more than merely doubled. I, and so many women I know, do not want just a bigger piece of the patriarchal pie. *We want to change the recipe, improve the nourishment and the taste.* We want to bring the new and fresh ingredients already bursting from our female hearts, hands, and experience. In 2003 Carl Sagan asked,

> Why is the half of humanity with a special sensitivity to the preciousness of life, the half untainted by testosterone poisoning, almost wholly unrepresented in defense establishments and peace negotiations worldwide?

"Men and women *are* different," wrote the English writer Virginia Woolf. "What needs to be made equal is the value placed on those differences." That's it. *Value.* Like a nickel is worth more than a penny. If a woman is seen as a penny and a man is seen as a nickel, our entire value system is impossibly skewed.

In his very inspiring book, *The Gender Knot*, Allan G. Johnson writes:

> A society is patriarchal to the degree that it promotes male privilege by being *male dominated, male identified,* and *male centered.* It is also organized around an obsession with control and involves as one of its key aspects the oppression of women.... If men occupy superior positions, it's a short leap to the idea that *men must be superior...* [and that] whatever men do will tend to be seen as having greater value.

As having greater value. That is certainly what Margaret Mead, the celebrated anthropologist, found. Years ago, I read that she had studied every group of humans available for study and observed that in every culture—if men wove the baskets, basket-weaving was given very high prestige—and if women wove the baskets, basket-weaving was given very low prestige. Nickels and pennies. I doubt that

Margaret Mead specifically studied the Mormons. But I have studied the Mormons, and I can verify that her conclusion covers us too.

I EXPERIENCE MORMONDOM to be a warm and beautiful and well-appointed home in which you suddenly find you're in a Patriarchy Funhouse that features crazy, rippling distortion mirrors built to magnify maleness and diminish femaleness. It's males who sit in the seats of authority, from God in his heaven on down to the leadership in Salt Lake City and out to every spot on the globe where Mormons congregate. It's males we pray to and pray through. It's males that preside at the pulpit. It's males that pray over and pass the sacrament, the tokens of the Lord's Supper, and officiate in all other ordinances. It's males (nearly always) whose portraits hang on the walls of our chapels and whose faces appear on the covers of our class manuals. It's males who pronounce every doctrine and policy from church headquarters. It's males we read about in most of the Old Testament and in ninety-nine percent of the Book of Mormon. (Thank you, Jesus of the New Testament, for being such a radical revolutionary, violating tradition, speaking of and to women, treating them as fully human.)

It's males we worship in song. In one very lovely hymn, in the midst of eight pronouns honoring the "he" and the "his" of masculine divinity, we sing, "The grave yield up *her* dead." The wounding contrast, lost on our consciousness, drops into our subconscious and subtly fuels the disparity of gender value in both male and female brains. I sometimes change the gender of words in hymn lyrics. I did that once when I was sharing a hymnbook with a young man I knew only slightly. The hymn was "Faith of our Fathers." By the time we got to the third verse he was enthusiastically singing along with me:

> Faith of our mothers, holy faith,
> We will be true to thee till death!

These are the Mormon rooms that we live in, walk in, worship in. These are the mirrors of distortion in which we, women and men, girls and boys, catch glimpses of ourselves, see our gender magnified or diminished. Many religious houses in our Judeo-Christian tradition share similar mirrors, and many are quietly going about the business of mirror replacement.

But there is a room in our church home that is unique to Mormons. The polygamy room. We know it's there, and we try not to talk about it, try not to even think about it. But something happens and we're suddenly in it and we can't avoid looking in those bizarre distortion mirrors: one man looming large—and two half-size women. Or maybe five very small women—one nickel and five pennies. The husband we are sealed to dies, we think about dating—and suddenly we are in that frightening room. We are a divorced Mormon man, believing we are eternally sealed to a woman we hope never to see again—and we're in the room. We marry a man sealed to a wife who died—and we're in the room. We are a father whose very own children, we have been told, are eternally sealed to the deceased husband of the wife and mother in our own home today—and we're in the room. Confusion all around. Rippling mirrors showing misrepresentations that no one can defend, no one can explain. We read Section 132 in our Doctrine and Covenants and we're in the room:

> If any man espouse a virgin, and desire to espouse another.... And if he have ten virgins given unto him by this law, he cannot commit adultery, for they belong to him...therefore is he justified. (D&C 132:61–62)

As we read that scripture, the mirror seems to undulate: one satisfied and looming man circled by ten tiny and confused women. A dime and ten pennies. We need some air. We feel dizzy, unbalanced. *Balance*—that's it! With every other flaw in polygamy there is this: visually, emotionally, spiritually, it is just bad design.

On the way out of that stifling room, we go through the kitchen and see that our visiting teacher, miraculously sensing that we are overwhelmed or ill or grieving, has snuck into the kitchen and disappeared without a word, leaving on the counter a full dinner for six: an irresistible chicken and shrimp casserole, a lentil-couscous salad, a loaf of warm whole-wheat bread with a jar of homemade raspberry jam, and a lemon meringue pie. The note, hand-made and featuring dried flowers, reads: "YOU ARE LOVED."

MORMON WOMEN HAVE had a ragged history in terms of equality. Being treated with politeness, consideration, even respect is different from being treated as an equal. From where I sit, here is a very brief summary of the history of Mormon women in relationship to the institutional church. In early church history, women were set on a progressive track in a patriarchal institution, with the Prophet Joseph encouraging their participation as spiritually powerful beings, giving them significant authority and responsibilities and teaching that our divine source is both Father and Mother. This progressive track was immediately sabotaged by the arrival of polygamy, which added to the patriarchal paradigm a new and bewildering layer—in God's highest order the male (singular) is eternally central and the female (plural) is eternally auxiliary. Mormon women variously fought this assignment and complied with it, often remaining in many ways powerful individuals.

Numerous Utah women were deeply involved in the national fight for suffrage, and they greatly admired women like Susan B. Anthony, who visited Utah in 1895. In their *Women's Exponent*, they bemoaned the fact of her arrest for voting, and had scathing words for the country that would raise "the late slaves to the dignity of political sovereignty" and yet punish as criminals "a few of the most intelligent women in the country for exercising the right of political citizenship." Upon Anthony's death the Mormon women leaders mourned the passing of "humanity's uncrowned queen" and expressed a hope that after death they might "be permitted to mingle and labor...side by side with Susan B. Anthony."

Utah women were among the first to serve on juries and as superintendents of public instruction. Martha Hughes Cannon was the first woman in the nation to be elected a state senator, winning against her own husband, Angus, who ran on the opposite ticket. Leonard Arrington wrote that early Utah produced "the most remarkable group of women doctors in American history." In an issue of the *Woman's Exponent* in 1872 was a report of two Utah women who were admitted to the bar, and on the next page was a note that the first woman lawyer on the Pacific Coast was refused admission to the bar of Santa Cruz, California. Through the Relief Society, Utah women managed impressive ventures, among them the "Wheat Project," dedicated to helping the poor and needy. Entirely independent from the men, the women bought and planted and raised and harvested and sold and donated enormous quantities of wheat. Some of their grain made its way to California in 1906, sent to help the survivors of the San Francisco earthquake. In 1933, they wrote in their *Relief Society Magazine* that looking at the names of women holding responsible political positions made it appear even probable that there might one day be a woman president of the United States.

At the turn of the century and through the first decades of the 1900s, the power that Mormon women had evidenced within the institutional church became gradually diminished by a growing emphasis on spiritual leadership by the male priesthood. Still, the leaders of the Relief Society and individual strong women held a solid presence in the church and ran the women's organization with a great deal of autonomy. Relief Society meetings were rich with thoughtful lessons created by women and geared to women's interests and needs.

And then came the Priesthood Correlation Program, a church-wide reassignment of leadership power, completed in 1972, intended to provide consistency and uniformity of doctrine, policy, and programs. Women, who had in some ways been able to act independently or sometimes as partners in church leadership, came to be firmly under the stewardship of men. Representative of this loss of power was the fate of the Wheat Program. After its 100-year existence as a singularly female enterprise, it was incorporated into the church's welfare fund. In 1978 President Barbara Smith relinquished over 226,291 bushels of Relief Society wheat, worth $1,651,157, as well as other assets that totaled three-quarters of a million dollars. Mormon sociologist Armand Mauss wrote that "correlation" resulted in "a reduction in the power and autonomy of women."

IT IS MY business to tell the stories. That something had gone terribly wrong is clear from a few of the many events I wrote into the pages of my diary.

April 19, 1976

Yesterday [a co-worker at BYU Motion Picture Studio] came by…[and] told me that recently they showed the first cut of [*The First Vision*] to some of the Brethren. In the film is a nice shot of the family around the table—it pans from Joseph Smith Senior around the others to Joseph and his mother at the end of the table. She reaches over and gives Joseph a warm squeeze on his arm. Thomas Monson's reaction to this: "Why did you feature the mother? We've got to feature the father. This is a priesthood-oriented church. We've got to feature the priesthood, not the mother."

March 11, 1986

[A friend at the highest level of leadership in the Relief Society] called me the other day. She said that to her observations "things are worse for women now than they've been at any time in the history of the church." She said the lessons in Relief Society are obviously written by men for what they want women to be, that the meat and the challenging thinking that used to be in the lessons is gone now.

Visiting England on a book tour for *Goodbye, I Love You,* I
wrote:

March 10, 1987

I had received a letter inviting me to dinner from Wendell Ash-
ton, mission president in London. He used to be editor of the
Deseret News and then head of Church Public Communica-
tions. His wife, Belva, is a good woman whom I had talked to on
several occasions about our mutual concerns regarding women
in the church. [On February 7, 1977, I had asked her, "What do
you see as the future for women in the church?" She said, "Well,
I'll tell you, Carol Lynn. I think we've hit the bottom, and the
only way now is up."].... Belva called me back and invited me
to stay with them for my second week in their flat. I gratefully
accepted....

I must write down some of the things Belva and I talked
about. I won't write down everything, as certain things should
remain private. But my commitment to history showing the
fuller picture is very important to me, and so I'm going to write
down some things.

Belva was on the General Board of the Relief Society for
a long time, and saw the whole thing deteriorate as Correlation came in and put the R.S. down further and further on the
charts. It was happening at the end of Belle Spafford's reign....
[She remembered Belle saying to the Board when she saw the
damage: "They closed us down. They've closed down the Relief Society."] And when Barbara Smith took over she had not
much power. The budget was taken out of the hands of the R.S.,
they could not call their own counselors...could not have control over their own lessons, lost the R.S. magazine, etc, etc.

Seeing how crippled they were as leaders, Belva and Alice Smith offered to write a letter to the Brethren, telling them
how they viewed all that had happened and asking for some
concessions. Barbara agreed and sent the letter over to their ad-
visors (some of the Twelve [Apostles], some Seventies). Barbara
was called in (by one of the Seventies whose name she would
not give me) and he "tore her apart." He told her never, never
to do anything like that again. Barbara went back to her office and locked the door and sobbed and sobbed. She didn't go
home. Her husband called that evening and she didn't answer

the phone. Finally he went to her office and found her just devastated. Belva was very sad and bitter about all this.

The women of the Mormon Church had it underlined for them and were told not to forget that they are auxiliary. Important and useful, but auxiliary. A letter I wrote to the President of the church, Gordon B. Hinckley (with copies to the Quorum of the Twelve, general Relief Society Presidency, Office of Curriculum Planning, and my stake and ward leaders) contained this:

January 12, 2003

As I sat in sacrament meeting this morning, I took the occasion to read the first lesson in the new Priesthood/Relief Society manual. No woman I have ever talked to has been pleased that we have increasingly been offered manuals written more and more for men and less and less for women. But we continue to hope.

This morning, as I read the first lesson and examined the entire text, I remembered the old English law of marriage that said when male and female join together they become one, and the one is him. I felt I was holding in my hands an anachronism. How can we be at this level of consciousness in the year 2003?

Today millions of excellent, faithful LDS women are given a lesson called "The Origin and Destiny of Mankind." In the entire nine pages of this lesson, there are two occurrences of words that acknowledge the female, "forefathers and mothers," "sons and daughters." There are dozens of references to our being sons of God and being asked to comprehend our dignity and manhood. I propose that it is unacceptable that today we ask a woman to teach women from a book that is exclusively the thoughts of men and in a presentation that is almost entirely for men.

As of this writing, nothing has changed significantly regarding these male-centric manuals. Seized by nostalgia, I just went down to my storage room and picked up a handful of Relief Society magazines preserved by my ancestors in Dingle, Idaho. Opening the first one, October of 1932, I find a Literature Lesson on "Faust" by

Goethe. Here's a lesson called "The Difference between Education and Indoctrination." We could use that one today. And here's an issue with an intriguing cover—a large bronze statue of a pioneer woman on a horse, cape flowing, a man with a rifle walking beside, created by a famous New York sculptor. I love the look of this magazine. I love to run my fingers over the cover. It feels like a woman dropping by for a delicious visit with another woman.

And paradoxically, despite institutional status and power having been taken away from women, Mormon women still are powerful beings, finding important ways to serve in their families, in the world, and in their church, enjoying tremendous opportunities for education, for development and sharing of talents, for leadership training, for public speaking and teaching. Brilliant individual Mormon women and impressive organizations created by Mormon women are making a difference in the world. One, out of the dozens I could mention, is a woman I have corresponded with but have yet to meet, Becky Douglas, a suburban housewife from Atlanta. In 2000, Becky responded to a godly impulse to help the children of leprosy victims in India. At this writing, her "Rising Star Outreach" is internationally known for its amazing work in helping leprosy colonies become more healthy, educated and self-supporting communities. It is no surprise to find a Mormon woman behind a large good.

Still, within the church institution itself, there remains for women a tension that is always there—powerful/subordinate. It leads, I think, to some unhealthy emotions and behaviors. A contemporary Mormon scholar, Claudia Bushman, writes in a recent issue of *Exponent II* (an important periodical for Mormon women's voices), that except for one "huge move forward for women—lowering the missionary age for girls, I would say that there has been a net loss of opportunity and responsibility for women in the church in the last 40 years." This is not lost on today's young women, who in many ways feel of equal value in their world and in many ways feel of lesser value in their church. Not many years ago. President Gordon B. Hinckley read in general conference a letter from a young girl that said something like, "Why does God love boys more than girls?" Of course he assured the girl that she was mistaken, that our Heavenly Father loves his children equally.

LONG AGO, HUMANITY shifted scientific theory from the Ptolemaic system (the earth at the center of the solar system) to the Copernican system (the sun at the center of the solar system). I yearn for the paradigm shift that moves male-female relationship theory from the patriarchal system (the male at the center of the universe with the female orbiting around him) to the partnership system (male and female dancing in perfect balance at the center of the universe). No one is personally harmed by the fiction that the earth is the center point of everything, but this other fiction—the fiction that maleness is central and femaleness auxiliary—this affects the daily life of every woman and every man that it touches and leaves us disoriented, many of us displaced and disheartened, and some of us seriously abused.

In our small Mormon universe, I submit that the first *large* step toward that better day—not the good but small steps of allowing women to pray in General Conference, letting female leaders sit on the stand in church meetings, putting female portraits up in the halls, placing women leaders more solidly on high committees, giving women leaders a central place in an impressive church-sponsored refugee-assistance program, putting in place new emphasis on the history of women in the church, and certainly not more talks assuring us all that women are special and must be respected—the first *large* step has got to be disassembling the paradigm of polygamy. That pattern functions as a unique and sad overlay to ordinary, run-of-the-mill patriarchy, and seeps through as a powerful glue that holds firmly in place the fiction of male centrality. In the poignant words of a woman who sent me her story:

I was raised in a conservative Mormon household, and I remember sharing my thoughts about polygamy with my mother. The desperate inequality inherent in a system that makes me one of many, but requires that my husband is my center-of-orbit was so heart-wrenching.

I remember the pained look on the face of my mother, who loved the LDS Church dearly, when she told me that she thought most women have to grapple with this doctrine eventually. My sister, aunt, mother, and I would discuss this matter at length, trying to come up with rationales, all the while disguising the obvious wounds the doctrine caused us.

I would leave the church years later. Polygamy was a doctrine that haunted my lasting happiness, the "worm at the core" of peace and love that I otherwise felt from the gospel. A culture that teaches men to acquire women for their own exaltation treats them like chattel, something to be owned or possessed, not valued as respected persons. That women's feelings on this doctrine have been so routinely ignored is reflective of how little we value women as humans.

We may say we value women, but what we mean is we love their service, we want their sacrifice. We don't want their wholeness and their perspectives and their humanity.

I WANT TO end this chapter with a better vision, a story that involves one of the many, many Mormon men in my world who are ready to help create a Partnership Zion. A few years ago a man who was serving in our stake presidency, and who I admired enormously, emailed to ask my help. He was preparing a talk to give at "stake priesthood meeting" to a large group of men on the subject of creating "roundtables" at church in which a true partnership of men and women could participate together, and he knew I had given a lot of thought to these issues. For a couple of weeks we had a great exchange—me sending him ideas and material and him responding with excitement and appreciation. Afterwards, when he sent me a copy of his talk, I was pleased to see he had quoted Riane Eisler as saying, "Just as one cannot sit in the corner of a round room, as we shift from a dominator to a partnership society, our old ways of thinking, feeling, and acting will gradually be transformed." And I was especially delighted to see that he had closed his talk with the great story I had sent him from the book *Half the Sky* by Nicholas Kristof and Sheryl Wudunn, the first husband-wife team to win a Pulitzer Prize for journalism, a story called "The Miracle of Rwanda." It is worth the space to tell it here, and it still thrills me that a few hundred Mormon men heard this from one of their leaders.

> Rwanda is an impoverished, landlocked, patriarchal society that still lives in the shadow of the 1994 genocide in which 800,000 people were slaughtered in one hundred days.... Yet somehow from this infertile, chauvinistic soil has emerged a country in which women now play an important economic, political, and social role—in a way that hugely benefits Rwanda as a whole. Rwanda is consciously implementing policies that empower and promote women—and, perhaps partly as a result, it is one of the fastest-growing economies in Africa. In some respects, in everything but size, Rwanda is now the China of Africa.
>
> In the aftermath of the genocide, 70 percent of Rwanda's population was female, and so the country was obliged to utilize women. But it was more than necessity. Men had discredited themselves during the genocide. Women were just minor players in the slaughter, so that only 2.3 percent of those jailed for the killings were female. As a result, there was a broad sense afterward that females were more responsible and less inclined to savagery. The country was thus mentally prepared to give women a larger role.
>
> Paul Kagame, the rebel leader who defeated the genocidaires and became Rwanda's president, wanted to revive his country's economy and saw that he needed women to do that. "You shut that population out of economic activity at your peril," he told us, as his press secretary—a woman—looked on approvingly. "The decision to involve women, we did not leave it to chance," he added. "In the constitution, we said that women have to make up 30 percent of the parliament."
>
> Kagame...regularly has appointed strong women to cabinet posts and other top positions. Women now hold the positions of president of the supreme court, minister of education, mayor of Kigali, and director of Rwanda television, while at the

grassroots level many women played major roles in village re-
construction.... In September 2008, a new election left Rwanda
the first country with a majority of female legislators—55 percent in the lower house.... Rwanda is also one of the least corrupt, fastest-growing, and best-governed countries in Africa.

WHEN EACH INDIVIDUAL is free to create a life that is driven by
unique talent and dreams as well as by gender, we will know we are
in the vicinity of partnership. When the major decisions of nations,
institutions, businesses, churches, families feel as if they came from
long consideration by the elders of the tribe, female and male, sitting
in a large circle and asking, *what is best for the children?—what is
best for the seventh generation?—what is best for all?*—we may have
entered that Promised Land.

In my own Mormon culture, we will have evicted the Ghost of
Eternal Polygamy. I know this because I know my Mormon people,
and we are better than to let this sad situation go on much longer.
The Ghost will hold no purchase with us, and in the new and accurate mirrors of our spiritual home we will see the truth—one man
and one woman standing side by side, equal in value—nickel for
nickel, dollar for dollar, priceless soul for priceless soul.

I don't pretend to know precisely how things will *look* in Mormondom as a place of partnership. But I know how they will *feel.* Let
us revisit those powerful words of Maya Angelou: "...People will
forget what you said, people will forget what you did, but people will
never forget how you made them feel." Once the Ghost is banished
from Mormondom, many fine things can fall into place. On some
good day we will have a church in which it is just as likely that a little
boy will write the prophet and say, "Why does God love girls more
than boys?"—as that a little girl will write the prophet and say, "Why
does God love boys more than girls?" And when the thought never
occurs to either boys or girls, women or men, that one gender seems
favored of the church, seems favored of God—when we know and
feel in the depth of our hearts that both genders are equally valued by

the Divine Parents who are equally valued by us—then we will know that this is the place, that we have indeed created a Partnership Zion.

Other Voices:

"Gender inequality in the church clouds almost everything for me"

When I met and got to know the man who would be my husband, I was thrilled. I was in deep, serious love and we were an amazing fit. Surely we would have an eternally happy and equal union.

But then the plot thickened. When he and I first went to the temple a week or so before our marriage, I heard some phrases that clearly placed me in a subordinate position to my husband, and I thought—perhaps polygamy really *would* be required at some point, and therefore my life with my husband would not be "just the two of us"—and this for all eternity!

I was soul-sick as these thoughts took over. After that temple session, as we sat together in the parking lot and I sobbed uncontrollably, he listened to my distress and—for the first time in his life, I think—began to realize how hard it can be to feel equal as a woman in the church.

Finally he said, "Do you know that God loves you just as much as he loves me?"

"Yes," I replied.

"Then do you realize that means that you will have every happiness that I will?"

It was a few weeks later, on our way to our wedding reception in his hometown, that I brought up the specific topic of polygamy. As wonderful as our first week as newly marrieds had been, polygamy and the accompanying idea that heaven might actually consider me as an appendage to rather than an equal partner with my husband had nevertheless left me feeling defeated, depressed, and even desperate. After the dam broke loose and I cried for a few minutes, I finally shared with him the questions that had plagued me over the last few weeks: Was he guaranteed all of me for eternity, while I only had part of him?

What if I die first?—I would have no say in whether he got sealed to another woman. What if he dies first?—would he get with another woman in heaven before I got there? How could I ever truly feel safe and at ease in our relationship—like I wasn't in a never-ending competition for his affections and loyalty—with the polygamy doctrine always hanging over my head.

My dear husband, who loved me so much and who took my struggles seriously, could only hold me and tell me again and again that I was the only girl he wanted to be with, now and forever.

I hear that from him now on a daily basis, but there are still those fears about things he and I cannot control. Polygamy, while rarely talked about openly, is still everywhere in the church. It's in our family history. It's in the history of the church. There's no way to hide the fact that Joseph Smith married a number of women and was sealed to them for eternity, even women who were already married to other men. There's Emma and the betrayal she felt from his deception.

I believe that Joseph was a prophet, but I also believe Joseph made mistakes—serious mistakes—and that polygamy was one of those. "By their fruits ye shall know them," and the fruits of polygamy have not been good. I choose to have faith that things will get better for Mormon women regarding how we are allowed to view ourselves and our eternal futures.

Polygamy in the eternities is the church's elephant in the room, in the chapel, in the temple. That teaching, along with other things that treat women as though they are less than men, was the major factor in my leaving the LDS Church. Mormon polygamy would never have been practiced, and would not be expected in eternity, if there always were six female and six male apostles.

Women have an unequal standing with men in our family hierarchy. The ongoing legacy of polygamy in Mormonism breeds sexism, shame, confusion, fear, feelings of deep inadequacy in many women, and feelings of entitlement in men. I'm not sure how much longer I can be in a church that perpetuates this idea of women as property.

My story is of my sweet baby sister. As I write this, she is packing up to leave her verbally and physically abusive husband who is again away somewhere high on prescription drugs. She and her husband and their new baby were sealed in the temple three years ago. She is filing for divorce.

When all is said and done, he will be able to get sealed to another woman (if he temporarily cleans up his act) in the temple and she is left powerless, even though he's the one 100 percent in the wrong here. If she remarries, it's up to her ex-husband if he gives her permission to break the sealing. So there's a good chance her future children will not be sealed to their actual father but to this first husband, an abusive guy they may never know. All because she's a woman. This doctrine has already caused our family so much pain. The only hope we have is that we got it wrong and God does not behave that way, even though our church does.

As an adolescent male teen, I found the thought of multiple sex partners very cool and sexually arousing when I learned about polygamy in seminary. Adult maturity gave an understanding of the unfairness polygamy brings to the woman, because it makes her a status symbol and the "property" of a man. Women are to be collected—and maybe even traded—like baseball cards.

I am a life-long, temple-attending, active, male member of the church. Polygamy is the subject that makes me saddest, angriest, and most bewildered. The inherent sexism and unfairness of it contradicts most of the core doctrines of love, charity, and the worth of "each soul" that I cherish. The thought of eternal polygamy diminishes my hope for the afterlife, my trust in the LDS depiction of God, my interest in family history and temple work, and my faith in the church itself.

As a woman who was sexually abused as a child, I grew up with beliefs about being unimportant, unworthy, unclean, and used. When I learned of polygamy and what really happened back in church history, the feelings of abuse came back very strong. I would cry and get angry. I couldn't go to church for a while, just in case our lesson was on Brigham Young, or polygamy, or church history. I would get so angry and anxious and sad, I couldn't get through the rest of my day.

I was partly downright pissed at these women who so willingly agreed to polygamy. I was angry at the women and men who supported it, who contributed to sexual inequality, and angry that my children and I are affected by it today. I was (and still am) angry that many men still believe they are naturally entitled to women because they are simply men of the church. It is truly disgusting that men (my husband a prime example) are taught that one day on earth or in the eternities, they will need to be prepared to take on more wives.

The inequality of gender roles in the church clouds almost everything for me right now. Male privilege nearly always trumps female need. Am I to play second fiddle not only in this life but in the life to come? Polygamy and the church's sealing practice suggest that. My dissatisfaction seems to increase as my husband has more time-intensive callings (he is currently serving as the bishop of our ward). I have flat-out told him that if there is polygamy in the next life, and we are supposed to be a part of it, I'm gone. I would choose hell. And he believes me.

The leadership of the church would do well to fully disclose the reasons for the sealing practices and acknowledge that they absolutely imply eternal polygamy. As a current "Mission President's Wife," I felt like a liar last week when I told an investigator that the blessings of the temple are the same for everyone. They are not.

My experience with LDS doctrine as it relates to women was extremely negative. I never felt that I was encouraged to be an individual in the church. Quite the contrary, I was much preferred as a quiet and obedient face in the crowd. I believe this is also the function of polygamy: it encourages women to be subservient to one man and keep the peace.

I always got the sense that the law of polygamy didn't bother the men in my life as much as it bothered me because deep down they felt it was kind of an awesome, sexual thing that benefited them. Much like Muslims and their promise of seventy-two virgins.

I know many women, myself and my mother included, who have fought and cried with their husbands because our heaven came with the depressing subtext that we will have to share our husband. It does not feel like equality at all. It feels like being a possession. Polygamy started in ancient tribes where men treated their women like property, and that our church carries it on today is ridiculous and shameful, and it makes me angry. What kind of God would think this up? Not one I want to worship or adore, I can tell you that.

The inequality in positions of "authority" between women and men, combined with the assumption by many that polygamy is coming back one day, can invite terrible abuses. I am close to and have spoken at length with a young woman and her father and mother, all three of whom told me this story:

In the early 80s the father received a phone call from his daughter, who was serving a mission in Australia. When she finally could speak through her hysterical sobs, the daughter said, "Dad! Did the prophet reveal that polygamy is back? Our mission president said that polygamy is back!"

Forty-eight hours later two General Authorities arrived in Sydney. A few hours after that the mission president was on his way home to Utah and to an excommunication. He had privately courted eight of the twelve sister missionaries, conducting "interviews" with them for hours, praying with them, reading scriptures about eternal marriage, and revealing to them that he was to be their husband. A number of the sisters had believed him and had become sexually involved with him. My young friend was the first to push back and to expose this abuse. Elder Thomas Monson, one of the two General Authorities to respond, praised her courage. [This incident has also been reported on podcasts by several Elders who were serving at that time in Australia.]

I am fifteen years old. I have struggled a lot in church for the past few years because I have conflicting feelings toward temple marriage and sealing. My stomach churned the first time I heard about eternal polygamy. And you know what? I refuse to believe it. The thought is disgusting and outrageous, and I refuse to believe that a loving Heavenly Father would have anything to do with something so unjust, so sexist, so unequal and objectifying as polygamy. I believe that if we push for this to stop, we can make it stop. Please be brave, and never stop fighting for equality.

I have always had the satisfaction of seeing truth triumph over error, and darkness give way before light.

—Joseph Smith

Change takes but an instant. It's the resistance to change that can take a lifetime.

—Hebrew Proverb

-11-

Toward a Partnership Future

MY BUSINESS IS to tell the stories, and I have told them. But it is a poor storyteller who leads us into a dark alley and does not point toward the light. And so I see that something else is also my business. I must share my hopes, my vision of how things will look and will feel when we acknowledge that some things have gone wrong on gender issues in the Mormon corner of the world that God made and accept the call to put those things right.

Brother Joseph taught that all things were created spiritually before they were created physically. I think we do this daily, creating in our minds what will soon be tangible, or as Albert Einstein put it: "Imagination is everything. It is a preview of life's coming attractions." That is why I write this book, and why I must not end before I articulate as clearly as I can the vision I hold, and that I believe many of you hold. Sharing words and images, we are creating on the level of mind a Partnership society. Spirit into matter. Wave into particle.

I'm told that the mills of the gods grind slowly. This I do not believe. I believe the mills of the men grind slowly in this trudging, bureaucratic world of ours. I believe that the thoughts of God travel more quickly than lightning and that revelation strikes each one of us daily. Once we Mormons are truly aware of a need we can be quick to address it. Even if we caused it. When, in 1856, Brigham received word of the people in the handcart companies dying on the plains, he did not hesitate. His mind and heart said, "Emergency!" and within hours rescue wagons with food and clothing were on their way. The thousands of women and men today whose suffering is caused by the Ghost of Eternal Polygamy deserve that we act and act quickly.

In 2009 FORMER President Jimmy Carter severed his relationship of six decades with the Southern Baptist Church because of its rigid stance against the equality of women. He said in a TED talk in 2015 that a major contribution to the ongoing worldwide abuse of women and girls is that in general "men don't give a damn," that men may say they don't believe in discrimination against women and girls, but still they "enjoy a privileged position" that's hard to give up, especially for "the majority of men who control the university system…control the military system…control the governments of the world…and control the great religions." My personal experience in Mormondom is not that most men "don't give a damn," but that most men do not understand. They have seen only through the dark glass of patriarchy and cannot yet envision the new world. And so it is up to us, women and girls, to be the messengers, the teachers and the guides. In this we help prepare our people for that new world in which God, the divine alchemist, will take the base metal of the "sins of the fathers" and turn it into gold.

Here are my beliefs regarding what must and will happen to achieve a Mormon future that is truly post-polygamy:

BELIEF # 1. A couple who chooses to marry in the temple can go into that holy place and stand on equal ground. Man and woman will know that they are of equal status in the eyes of God and in the eyes of the church. They are partners. Regardless of any sealing to a prior spouse, they are identical in status and in opportunity. The words spoken in the ceremony assure them that their relationship is blessed to be an eternal one, dependent only upon their love, the will of the Lord, and their eternal agency. The woman does not give herself in marriage any more than the man gives himself. Both fully give and fully receive. Any concern about a past or future relationship is laid to rest in the knowledge that God's great design is larger than we can map with our charts and forms, our erasures and additions, and is far, far more brilliant and benevolent. The extended families of both bride and groom have cause only to rejoice, for there are no winners or losers.

There is precedent for this hope. In his memoir, *An Abundant Life,* Hugh B. Brown, counselor in the First Presidency under President David O. McKay, said that he discussed at length with President McKay the problems resulting from the remarriage of a woman, sealed to a husband who had died, desiring to be sealed to a second husband so that they could create a family with their own children. President Brown suggested a solution to President McKay, who followed it and "permitted several women to be sealed to two men, saying, 'Let the Lord straighten it out when they get to the other side.'"

BELIEF #2. Section 132 of the Doctrine and Covenants will receive an "inspired revision" with plural marriage removed from the cannon so that women and girls will be spared the wounding to our femaleness that we receive today. We will no longer take from those pages the deeply troubling understanding that we are objects for the use of men and that if our husband desires, on earth or in heaven, to take an additional ten virgins through the law of plural marriage, "they belong to him, and they are given unto him; therefore is he justified," and that if we are not willing to be obedient to this law we "shall be destroyed, saith the Lord," just as Emma Smith was threatened if she was not obedient.

Again, there is precedent for making such changes in our discourse, even in what we hold as scripture, with the specific purpose of being more accurate, more generous in our regard for a portion of humanity. A hymn that for decades was sung in tribute to the Prophet Joseph had in it these words:

> Long shall his blood, which was shed by assassins,
> Stain Illinois while the earth lauds his fame.

In 1927 when a new hymnal was published, the last line was changed to "Plead unto heav'n while the earth lauds his fame." This occurred as a result of the "Good Neighbor" policy the church was implementing to the broader country, and specifically as a gesture not to offend the good people of Illinois.

In 1971, the words, "And the red untutored Indian / Seeketh here his rude delights" were dropped from a hymn that we still sing titled "For the Strength of the Hills." And in 1985, a word in a hymn on missionary work that referred to non-members as "heathens" was changed to "nations."

Sadly, however, only a minimal amount of consideration has been given as to how the lyrics of our hymns represent and affect women. A male researcher observed that, even though some words were changed to be more gender inclusive when our current hymnal was published in 1985, the words in general were still heavily male, hymns listed specifically for male voices were twice the number of hymns listed for female voices, and while there were three more instances of "her" than "his" in our hymns, each instance of "her" referred not to female humans but to inanimate objects or concepts: Zion, Babylon, the earth, the grave. He further reported:

> I was surprised to find that the ratio of male gender-exclusive language to female gender-exclusive language was 147 to 2.... I look forward to a time when my wife, daughters, and mother can sing hymns in which they appear directly, not by inference, so that their sense of value as individuals may be increased.

Changes in doctrine are reflected in our hymns as well. The very strange "Adam-God" theory taught by Brigham Young—that the Adam of the Garden of Eden was in fact Michael the Archangel, who was in fact God the Father—after 145 years and considerable conflict, was officially pronounced "false doctrine" and finally taken out of the hymn book. "Sons of Michael" is still sung, but the original words, "That the Ancient One may reign / In his Paradise again!" were long ago changed to "That the ancient one doth reign / In his Father's house again!"

MUCH MORE WEIGHTY than changes to hymns is changes to scripture itself. But here, too, there is precedent. A linguistic challenge presented in the Book of Mormon involves what appears to be racist language. The less righteous group of people in that history, called Lamanites (historically identified as indigenous peoples of the Americas and Polynesia), are cursed by God with "a skin of blackness." In the first edition of the book in 1830, these Lamanites were promised that at a future time of righteousness "...they shall be a white and a delightsome people" (2 Nephi 30:6). As reported by a review at the apologetic FairMormon website:

> In 1840 the Book of Mormon was "carefully revised by the translator" Joseph Smith and in that edition the words "white and delightsome" were changed to "pure and delightsome...." Unfortunately for subsequent LDS interpreters, following the Prophet's death, the changes in the 1840 edition of the Book of Mormon were not carried over into subsequent LDS printings, which were based upon the edition prepared by the Twelve

Apostles in Great Britain. Consequently, Latter-day Saints did not reap the benefit of the Prophet's clarification until it was restored in the 1981 edition of the Book of Mormon.

Additionally, in 2010, the LDS Church made some similar changes in chapter summaries and some footnotes. One such change is in the summary of Mormon, chapter 5, which previously read, "the Lamanites shall be a dark, filthy, and loathsome people," and now reads, "because of their unbelief, the Lamanites will be scattered, and the Spirit will cease to strive with them."

I SUGGEST THAT the representation of women deserves a much higher consideration in our religious discourse. When words are presented as if they come directly from God, they can have monumental impact on our psyches, our spirits, our hearts, and our relationships. Women are given, in story at least, first place in the lifeboats, but often in more common circumstances we are consigned to the back of the bus.

You have read in this book many comments from today's LDS women about their experiences with the scripture on which plural marriage is based, such as, "*I remember sobbing in the bathroom of the seminary building when we studied Section 132 of the D&C.*" That image alone is a call to action. I believe the vast majority of LDS men and women will feel profound relief when a change is made so that women's hearts are no longer routinely broken when they read the pages of this scripture. Today church leaders acknowledge that "there have been times when members or leaders in the church have simply made mistakes." FairMormon has on its website, specifically referring to the Doctrine and Covenants:

> The Saints have never believed in inerrant prophets or inerrant scripture. The editing and modification of the revelations was never a secret; it was well known to the Church of Joseph's day, and it has been discussed repeatedly in modern church publications....

On behalf of my sisters and my brothers who are suffering to-day, I hope our capacity for correction, for "ongoing revelation," will rapidly come into play on the subject of polygamy.

THE HISTORY OF Section 132 is instructive. This section did not appear in print as part of the Doctrine and Covenants until 1876 when it replaced Section 101, which first appeared in 1835 as a denial that the church practiced or believed in plural marriage. Section 132 maintained its place throughout the very tumultuous period in Utah when the Mormons, in severe conflict with the United States government, vociferously defended and then relented on polygamy as a lived part of their gospel in order to survive as a church and also to become a state in the Union.

In 1930, scholar James E. Talmage, a senior Apostle in the Quorum of the Twelve, was asked by the First Presidency of the church to "prepare a shortened version of the Doctrine and Covenants." It was not to be a substitute, but was presented as "selections comprising Scriptures of general and enduring value," leaving the impression that scripture and revelation are "fluid and adaptable to new circumstances." The book was published under the imprint of the LDS Church and titled, *Latter-Day Revelations: Selections from the Book of Doctrine and Covenants of the Church of Jesus Christ of Latter-day Saints.* A number of sections were trimmed or discarded. Section 132, the cornerstone scripture regarding plural marriage, was missing altogether. According to Talmage's biographer, James P. Harris, fundamentalist Mormons were outraged. Immediately church President Heber J. Grant ordered the book withdrawn from sale and the remaining copies "shredded to avoid further conflict with the fundamentalists."

I look forward to the day when the feelings of women are given the consideration that was given the feelings of the fundamentalists by LDS leaders who were not willing in 1930, and have been unwilling since, to give up the deeply hurtful concept of male privilege and female pain inherent in Section 132 of the Doctrine and Covenants.

BELIEF #3. The doctrine of plural marriage will be disavowed entirely and no longer considered the Word of God as pertains to history, the present, or the eternal future. The teaching will go the way of various other teachings in Mormonism that were presented as doctrine and considered by many to be doctrine, such as the "Adam-God" teaching, a disturbing "blood atonement" teaching, both clearly disavowed by more recent leaders, and the long-lived teaching of the inferiority of the Negro race which resulted in the well-known fact of black members being barred from the LDS priesthood and refused temple privileges.

Of particular interest to our subject is the ending of the decades-long "law of adoption" within four years of the ending of the practice of plural marriage. Both were ended by President Wilford Woodruff, the practice of polygamy in 1890 and the law of adoption in 1894. Church Historian Leonard Arrington felt that the desire to connect the entire human family as one led to both the law of adoption (men being sealed to elect men as sons) and to the principle of plural marriage (women being sealed to elect men as wives). In ending it, President Woodruff pronounced the law of adoption "an incorrect procedure." The description Leonard Arrington used for plural marriage was "an unintended consequence."

The ending of the priesthood ban on black men offers a ready example for a possible ending of the teachings on polygamy. The first is highly charged with racism, and the second is highly charged with sexism. Both take a class of people and place them in a lesser position. Both make the error of assuming that God gives special standing to white males. For a long time in history, black men and women were considered property. For a long time in history, women in general were considered property. Sadly, "chattel" is a word you read in this book more than once as contemporary Mormon women describe their feelings regarding the history and the future threat of polygamy.

Interestingly, our nation's battle against slavery and our nation's battle against polygamy played out simultaneously. In 1860, Abraham Lincoln became the first Republican president, running on a platform of ending the "twin relics of barbarism," slavery and polygamy. In 1862, he signed into law the Anti-Polygamy Act, which he failed to enforce as the Civil War took all of his attention.

In the more than one hundred years after slavery ended, the Mormons generally behaved the same as other groups of Americans in letting the barbarism of slavery move into less blatant and more subtle racism. But our Mormon reluctance toward full and official approval of equality for black people lasted longer than that of most groups. During the tumultuous days of the Civil Rights movement, the LDS Church held religiously to a tradition that mandated the exclusion of men of African descent from ordination to the priesthood and the exclusion of both black men and black women from temple privileges. Decades of grief resulted, during which the church experienced pointed criticism from without and painful conflict within.

On June 1, 1978, the President of the Church, Spencer W. Kimball, who had spent many hours alone in prayer and meditation in the Holy of Holies on the upper floor of the temple in Salt Lake City, called together his Twelve Apostles and carefully expressed his hopes that the ban could be lifted and asked them to join with him in prayer. Many of those present later gave accounts of profound spiritual experience that left no doubt in their minds that they were instructed to move forward in lifting the ban. For almost all LDS people as well as Mormon-watchers, this was very welcome news.

I'm sure it was the hope of church authorities that the lifting of the priesthood ban would be the end of concerns about race in the church. That did not happen. So many destructive and insulting teachings had been put in place—many of them utterances of men in the highest positions of authority—that serious racial problems continued to exist. Even into the twenty-first century, black members sometimes reported aloofness on the part of white members, such as a reluctance to shake hands with them or sit by them or even speak to them. Some of the repugnant teachings that continued to surface were that black people are descendants of Cain, that they were not valiant in the War in Heaven (the battle between good and evil, between Christ and Lucifer), and that skin color and righteousness are linked. The 1978 revelation had marked a change in church policy, but it had not repudiated the past.

Happily that changed in 2013. The church's official website had begun to publish straightforward, in-depth essays on a number of "Gospel Topics," historical and doctrinal, that had proved controversial. When the essay "Race and the Priesthood" was released in December of that year, it did something that had never been done before—it left a clear impression that the teachings around race, whose influence had been wide and deep, were not now—*and had never been*—correct. Specifically addressing those teachings, it states:

> Over time, Church leaders and members advanced many theories to explain the priesthood and temple restrictions.... [Some taught that] blacks descended from the same lineage as the biblical Cain, who slew his brother Abel...that God's "curse" on Cain was the mark of a dark skin...[that blacks were] less than fully valiant in the premortal battle against Lucifer and, as a consequence, were restricted from priesthood and temple blessings....
>
> Today, the Church disavows the theories advanced in the past that black skin is a sign of divine disfavor or curse, or that it reflects unrighteous actions in a premortal life; that mixed-race marriages are a sin; or that blacks or people of any other race or ethnicity are inferior in any way to anyone else. Church leaders today unequivocally condemn all racism, past and present, in any form.

The statement suggests the official ban on black men being ordained to the priesthood, read publicly by Brigham Young in 1852, was linked to "widespread ideas about racial inferiority." This was something Mormon ears had not heard before. This practice, long assumed to have been dictated by God, was instead Brigham Young acting from the racism of the day in which he lived? The more than a century of discrediting black men and women—all this was just a cultural thing based on an error? As historian Richard Bushman put it in an interview with the *Salt Lake Tribune*, the new statement

> drains the ban of revelatory significance, makes it something that just grew up and, in time, had to be eliminated…[and this] requires a deep reorientation of Mormon thinking. [If Brigham Young could make a serious error] it brings into question all of the prophet's inspiration. [Members need to recognize that God can] work through imperfect instruments. For many Latter-day Saints, that is going to be a difficult transition. But it is part of our maturation as a church.

Without question, the LDS community still has a long way to go regarding issues of race, but a vital page was turned with the unequivocal disavowal and condemnation of "all racism, past and present in any form."

THE GIVING UP of the other "relic of barbarism," polygamy, has a similar history but is not yet complete. Polygamy, which had for decades been preached and practiced by four LDS prophets and thousands of members as a God-given doctrine that would never change, finally did change. The United States government brought such crippling pressure that President Wilford Woodruff felt he had no choice. In 1890, he issued the "Manifesto," an official declaration of intent to cease plural marriages, which was ratified by a stunned and very divided membership. For years, chaos reigned as plural marriages continued to be secretly authorized by the highest authorities. Who knew what to believe? Very much as in Nauvoo, Mormon authorities said one thing publicly and another privately. In 1904, President Joseph F. Smith issued the "Second Manifesto," stating the church was no longer sanctioning marriages that violated the laws of the land and insisting that any Mormon who entered such a marriage would be excommunicated. Polygamy, alive on the underground, now had to dig into an even deeper underground, and then finally—in the mainstream LDS Church at least—had to settle for life as a Ghost content with promises that its power will be fully restored in God's heaven.

There are echoes of Nauvoo's and early Utah's double-speak around polygamy today. Plural marriage is routinely and officially dismissed as a thing of the past. President Gordon B. Hinckley said in essence on "Larry King Live": "Polygamy? That has nothing to do with us. We gave that up long ago." *Well, actually we did not. It's still active in our scripture, in temple sealings, and in the anticipation of what life will look like in the highest kingdom of heaven.*

Precisely like the insulting statements about the place of black men and women that were spoken and written in Mormon discourse for decades and continued to have life long after the 1978 priesthood and temple ban was lifted, the insulting statements and implications about the place of women have lived long after the Manifestos of 1890 and 1904, statements that break a woman's heart and leave a man confused. At this writing, about 5 percent of the active membership of the LDS Church is composed of black members. More than 55 percent of the active membership is composed of females. It is my profound hope and belief that soon women will be given the same consideration finally given to our black brothers and sisters.

The soft statements by church directives today that the Lord's standard for marriage is monogamy unless he directs otherwise are no match for what has been writ large and in granite in our history, our discourse, and our psyches for nearly two centuries. The electrifying, secret whispers of Joseph and the loud sermons of Brigham still echo through chapels, temples, homes, and hearts, assuring the Saints that we are not yet finished with polygamy.

THE FINAL DISMISSAL of the Ghost may come in a way that is similar to the dismissal of the priesthood ban and out of a similar acknowledgement of the prejudice of tradition. President Kimball said in an interview with the *Church News* regarding the intensity of his prayers prior to receiving the answer:

> I had a great deal to fight, of course, myself largely, because I had grown up with this thought that Negroes should not have the priesthood and I was prepared to go all the rest of my life till my death and fight for it and defend it as it was.

LEADERS AND MEMBERS alike have made the assumption that polygamy was and will be God's will for many of the righteous in eternity, and a significant number are likely prepared to "fight for it and defend it" to their death. I believe that assumption could change, as did the assumption of President Kimball about race. The correction around polygamy could happen soon and suddenly. Indeed, we could be struck by light, a Holy of Holies moment that brings both clarity and a commitment to act. Earlier in this book I wrote, "Whatever you believe about this man, do not think that Joseph did not love his people, never think that." I must say the same for Joseph's successors in the twenty-first century. They love their people and are committed to their happiness. They love the women of their church. They will not ignore this obvious pain.

It is my hope that soon we will read in the "Gospel Topics" section of the church's website—better yet hear read over the pulpit not to be missed by members of the church worldwide—that the doctrine of plural marriage truly has come to an end. There may be an explanation that mid-nineteenth century was a time of great religious and marital experimentation, that our early leaders were making various attempts at community and family organization that would last into eternity. I can imagine a few lines such as these that may parallel the disavowal of racism:

In Nauvoo and early Utah, church leaders and members advanced many theories to explain the presence of polygamy in our doctrine and practice. Some taught that it was mandated as a "restitution of all things," that it was essential to multiply and replenish the earth, or that it was necessary for highest glory in the eternities.

Today, the church disavows the theories and practices advanced in the past that a polygamous marriage is essential or advantageous for the highest level of exaltation—that in this life or in the next a man, but not a woman, may create more than one marriage relationship that is binding for eternity—that we have many Mothers in Heaven—and that a woman who refuses plural marriage is in danger of being destroyed. The anticipation of plural marriage in heaven is not correct doctrine and—along with the sexism inherent in that principle—is unequivocally condemned by the church.

THE BROTHER JOSEPH who I came to love and whom I love still would weep to see today's tears on this subject. He himself said, "I have always had the satisfaction of seeing truth triumph over error, and darkness give way before light." I believe satisfaction is what the eternal spirit of Brother Joseph felt as he saw the ending of the priesthood and temple ban. And I believe that satisfaction is what Brother Joseph will feel as he sees the departure of the Ghost of Eternal Polygamy. This departure is inevitable, I believe, because we will listen to the better angels of our nature, because we want to be not only on the right side of history but to be on the side of right, because polygamy bears bad fruit and has failed the test of Joseph's own words, of being "virtuous, lovely, of good report and praiseworthy." It has proved itself to be a destroyer. We—leadership, membership, women, men—all are better than to allow the pain and the stain of polygamy to remain on a church that is so vitally good, so profoundly strong in so many ways, and so demonstrably based on the principle of love taught by Jesus of Nazareth, by Brother Joseph, and by every other man and woman across the globe and across the centuries who grasped a spark of God and shared a godly message.

WHEN THE GHOST is finally banished, each young and tender girl will learn at church and at home that if she marries she will become the singular and full partner of a husband of her choice and that her divine nature and individual worth are such that she will never be "one of," here or in heaven. The writings and the folklore around polygamy, the old stories and the statements even of prophets, will have been put away in the drawer marked "expired," and will generate no more fear than ghost stories told around the campfire.

Every individual member of the church and every congregation will feel more open to the presence of our long-lost Heavenly Mother, for the disturbing Ghost has been evicted from both earth and heaven, and the glorious Goddess—full and sole Partner that she is in the creation and sustaining of life—is welcomed back into the family.

Marriages will be sweeter, with no holding back a piece of the heart just in case. A wife will sleep better, never startled in the night by the terrible thought, "…if I die before he does…." An elderly widow will spend her last days with peace of mind and no disquieting thought of "…I wonder if he has taken another wife already…." A husband will invest fully in his one and precious partner, with never a thought that she is not enough here or will be added to in heaven.

A widow will be able to mourn her loss, and then, if she wishes, look forward to a new relationship in which she can be seen as the desirable woman that she is, unobstructed by prior attachment. Her love for a past husband and a present husband do not conflict, for she knows that God is not asking her to make impossible choices, and that in heaven there will be many happy surprises.

A man who chooses to marry a widow will do so with full confidence that this is a blessed union and can only lead to good in this world and the next—for him, for her, for her children, his children, their children, and for her deceased husband. The entire family invests only in love and not in anxiety, confident that each relationship—wife to husband, sister to brother, mother and father to children—is secure.

The claim of our church that we create and support strong families will be even more true, as the ruptures and the tensions produced by the Ghost will have ceased. No one will experience apprehension over paperwork that plots out who will be with whom in heaven. All will breathe easily, confident that in the spectacular organization of the family of God, our Father and Mother in Heaven, all of us will receive, with each person we have loved and been loved by, a perfectly designed relationship, with eternal joy in good measure, pressed down, shaken together, and running over, a connection that our earthly minds cannot now begin to grasp.

And intertwined with every benefit will be the supreme one—the shedding of an old and debilitating distrust in a God that for many faithful LDS women and men has brought untenable spiritual and theological dissonance. A God who has prepared an eternity that will break the hearts of women and render them forever subordinate will be dismissed as preposterous. We will see with more clarity and with deeper appreciation the one in the mirror, the one on the other side of the bed, and the One who thought this all up in the first place. A new buoyancy will render us a stronger people, a people more prepared to gift the Lord with our portion of Zion.

WITNESS THE MYSTERY of transformation. Patriarchy has been spinning silk for its chrysalis. The process of deconstruction is underway. A shell breaks and a bright thing shivers. When the little butterfly of equality, of real partnership, begins to move her wings in Mormondom, a shift will be felt in far places. We are One, and when one is blessed, the blessing is for all. A woman in Ethiopia will refuse genital mutilation for her daughter. A girl in a desert of Afghanistan will bravely walk into a school for the first time. And in Osaka, a man for no apparent reason will decide against purchasing another girl for his brothel, and instead may find himself drawn to the fishing industry.

Religion isn't about believing things. It is a moral aesthetic, an ethical alchemy. It's about behaving in a way that changes you, that gives you intimations of holiness and sacredness.

—Karen Armstrong

God is love, and he that dwelleth in love dwelleth in God, and God in him.

—New Testament: 1 John 4:16

-12-
Joseph's Zion

I HAVE THIS fantasy. I play it out in my head whenever I get discouraged about religion, mine or anybody else's. Or sometimes just for fun. That fabulous moment at the opening ceremony of the Olympics, the parade of nations, when the athletes start pouring into the arena—those beautiful young people in costumes that celebrate their own country, waving their own flag, smiling from their heart, so thrilled to be there representing the people they love, giving their very best, watching each other give their best, everyone a good sport.

In my fantasy, it's a parade of religions, all come together to celebrate, to show their very best stuff, and to admire each other's best stuff. We enter the arena with banners showing the name by which we have been called, decorated with our special symbols. We're smiling and waving. We dress for tradition, for history, and local color. As we come in alphabetically, we're led by the Amish, and the rear is brought up by the Zoroastrians. We Latter-day Saints are right between the Jews and the Mennonites. This is a futurist fantasy. There are no medals. The only gold in evidence is the Gold of the Rule that every religious community rediscovered as it dug deep into its soul, that startlingly simple and indispensable law of compassion that is now treasured above all else. What was so often a platitude has become a platform for habitual action.

I know, I'm shamelessly optimistic. And because religion does not own the Gold in the Rule, in the larger narrative the unchurched and the atheists have also brought their own hearts and hands to creating "a new earth." But this particular story is of the religions. We've come together not to compete, but to share joy and to learn. *Here's what we have found that has proven to be godly. What have you found?*

I love it when the Latter-day Saints go marching in. I get to be in that number, and I couldn't be more pleased, smiling and waving. We've kept enough of our weirdnesses to make us interesting, but we've given up the things that were hurtful and did not measure up to the Rule that we take very seriously now.

Nobody preaches. We just share. I spend hours visiting the storytelling booths, those sacred little spaces unveiling the different faces of God. I sit quietly with the Buddhists, practice emptying my cluttered mind and courting enlightenment...*ommm...ommm*.... I watch in wonderment the drama, the spectacle, of the Catholics from early coarse morality plays to the splendor of the high mass. I come back again and again to the Quakers, resting in silence, purity, so grateful for their centuries of working for social justice.

At my own booth, the Mormon booth, I get to tell some really great stories. After all, it is my business to tell the stories. And after all, this is my fantasy. Few people even ask about polygamy now because it is well known that, truly, we gave it up long ago—completely and for real. We discovered in that great searching of the soul, as we burnished the Gold of our Rule into full brightness, that polygamy did not pass the test of compassion, of kindness, of seeing everyone as our own "kind." Once we embraced compassion with full clarity, giving up polygamy, root and branch, was not that hard. We tell Brother Joseph's stories of heaven, but I like best our stories of the here and now, and I tell them hoping Joseph might be listening.

WITH THAT THOUGHT, that powerful wish to tell Joseph...this fantasy morphs into a new one. I move out of the future into the past. June 23, 1844, just a few days before Joseph's death. I stand near the bank of the Mississippi River a few feet away from Joseph as he sits on a log close to the water. The Furies are closing in on him and he feels it. He has spent recent days sequestered in his office planning a strategy for survival. A warrant for his arrest for the destruction of the printing press...agitation all around...cries for his death...*a fair trial, is it possible?*...the night before, Saturday, crossing the swollen river to Iowa in a leaky boat, bailing out water with boots, Joseph, Hyrum, Willard, faithful Porter rowing...confusion on the other side...go to Washington to plead with President Tyler?...to the West to be followed by his people?...messages from Emma, from his friends...*don't leave us, come back, you promised never to leave us... Hyrum what shall I do?*...watching the city of Nauvoo come closer and closer as the boat rocks its way back again, back to...*like a lamb to the slaughter....*

Sunday, no day of rest...home at five in the afternoon. Chaos at the Mansion House. *I will go to Carthage in the morning...Governor Ford has promised protection!* Nine in the evening now and the full moon plays across the restless water. Familiar night sounds give Joseph a moment of calm...frogs and crickets...scent of pine and dogwood blossom. He would never have been able to have a moment alone that night, I know that, I'm making this up because I so want him to have a last few minutes to himself. At six-thirty tomorrow morning he will kiss his family goodbye for the last time, and he and Hyrum and the others will mount their horses.

I watch Joseph as he watches the racing river. Too fast, all is too fast. His mind is a constant prayer. *Bless my people…bless these my people…what will become of them?…bless Emma and the children…the thousands who heard the call and came…what of the work of Zion?… bless these my people….*

I remember the words of that song that was never sung in the movie that was never made:

Way down within us—where spirit is flowing—
There moves the dream—the vision, the knowing
That from the beginning God's breath was inside us—
There is no ending—not death can divide us.

Brothers and Sisters—hold out your hands.
Love one another 'til everyone stands
As Brothers and Sisters—sharing the sun—
Learning at last—that we are one.

Joseph is the prophet, but at this moment I know some things he does not know. I am a storyteller and there are stories I wish I could tell him. I would not tell him any of the sad stories, the painful stories that you have read in this book. He will learn of those soon enough. Tonight I would tell him a few stories that would cheer him. That godly spark, the spark he seized from the heavens and fanned into a dream of Zion, a place for the pure in heart, a home for the homeless where all are brothers and sisters…*sharing the sun… learning at last…that we are one…*I want to tell him that dream still lives…oh, imperfectly, but still it lives.

I would speak to Brother Joseph of our little Mormon corner of God's vast Zion. I would tell him that just as he organized and commissioned Emma and the women to go forth on the errand of angels, we women still go forth today. I would tell him the story of those dark days when my former husband Gerald, who went out to dream his impossible dream, lay dying of AIDS in my home where I was taking care of him…the ring of the telephone, Sister Spencer, my visiting teacher…*I'm not calling to ask if I can do anything for you…. I'm calling to tell you to put a pen and a notebook by your phone, and whenever anything occurs to you that needs to be done, write it down…. I will call at nine each morning and you will read me the list and the things will be done.* A godly impulse, quick to manifest because we had a system, and in that system we were sisters building Zion.

I would tell Joseph, too, about the time not long ago when my bishop—only a little older than Joseph himself tonight—said: *Sister Pearson, I have a calling for you.* I smiled. *I am a maverick, you know.* He smiled. *Of course I know…and you may be the only person in the ward who can do this particular thing.* I listened. *Certainly, Bishop, I will be happy to do that.* A few months, a few hearts and hands added to mine, and the large task he had given me was accomplished.

But the part of that story that I especially want Brother Joseph to hear is this small incident on the Sunday following the bishop's request. *Sister Pearson, will you meet with the bishop's counselors at four to be set apart for your new calling?* Fifteen minutes I was in the room with these two men, and when I left I was ashamed of myself. I had walked in humdrum, and I left with a bit of awe. Our systems are so smooth we can fail to see the splendor. *Two men, untrained lay clergy, moved to tears as they thanked me for things I had written that had blessed members of their families…then their hands on my head…words of confidence and power and blessing…a reminder of the value of the one soul I was called to serve….*

The thing is, we Mormons are *organized*. And we are committed by covenant to be a godly people. We've missed the mark a bunch of times and organized a few terrible things. Individually we stumble a lot. But the godly impulse still flows, like the river, moving around the rocks. When there is clarity, when we walk by the Rule, we are powerful. And what I want so urgently to say to Brother Joseph, here in these last moments as I watch him kneel beside the log and move his lips pleading not for his life but for his people, his work: *Joseph… Brother Joseph…the large and godly impulse you welcomed and embodied*

lives on...it has touched millions and it brings light...we are brothers
and sisters and we hold a vision of Zion...we bring our light, brightened
by your light...and we hold it high.

There are more stories, so many more, that I want to tell Joseph...but now he is standing...now he looks at the river for a final time...picks up a little stone and throws it far out into the water... now he turns and I hear the crunch of stick and pebble as he strides toward home.

I WILL CONTINUE to walk with the Saints and play my little part in the story. And when my part is finished and I'm in that higher, brighter place, I will still watch with interest. I will visit that Peering Window I made up, that hole in heaven that lets us see the whole of earth. Maybe Gerald and I will take an excursion there after our promised picnic. He and I are still sealed, you know, but Mormon authority is the least of it. We are sealed as friends forever by the matter of love and grief and loss and learning, that eternal learning that moves us ever toward God. Sister Emma will join us on occasion, I'm sure, and perhaps we may even have the honor of Brother Joseph's company as well. He liked nothing better than to be with his friends.

I will watch to see what may come of my own work. When the pioneers crossed the plains, often they planted seeds that would bring a harvest to those who came after—divine economy that brings peace to one who plants words.

I have told the stories.

I have shared my vision.

I am content.

Endnotes

INTRODUCTION

"Many things have gone wrong with the world that God made":
C.S. Lewis, *The Complete C.S. Lewis Signature Classics* (New York: HarperCollins, reprint edition, 2009), 41.

Statistics on ongoing abuse of women internationally:
U.N. Secretary-General's in-depth study on violence against women (2006), accessed September 20, 2015, http://www.refworld.org/docid/484e58702.html.

"Their women were incredible":
Wallace Stegner, *The Gathering of Zion* (Lincoln, Nebraska: University of Nebraska Press, 1992), 222.

"My business—Your business—God's business":
Byron Katie, *"The Work of Byron Katie,"* accessed December 2, 2015, http://thework.com/en.

Chapter Two: BROTHER JOSEPH

"An authentic religious genius, unique in our national history":
Harold Bloom, *The American Religion: The Emergence of the Post-Christian Nation* (New York: Simon and Schuster, 1992), 95.

"Praise to the man who communed with Jehovah!":
William W. Phelps, *Hymns of the Church of Jesus Christ of Latter-day Saints* (Salt Lake City: The Church of Jesus Christ of Latter-day Saints, 1985), 27.

"Book of Mormon as one of the 100 most influential "Books that Made America":
Library of Congress, accessed November 11, 2015, http://www.read.gov/btsa.html.

"In the full flush of classic hubris":
Eugene England, "Joseph Smith and the Tragic Quest," in
Dialogues with Myself: Personal Essays on Mormon Experience
(Midvale, Utah: Orion Books, 1984), 12. Available at:
http://signaturebookslibrary.org/dialogues-with-myself-01/.

"The Prophet lived his life in crescendo":
Joseph Fielding Smith, comp., *Teachings of the Prophet Joseph Smith* (Salt Lake City: Deseret Book Company, 1976), 356.

Greek Chorus speaks:
Rex Warner, translator, *Three Great Plays by Euripides* (New
York: The New American Library, 1958), 31.

"George A., I love you as I do my own life":
Hyrum L. Andrus and Helen Mae Andrus, comps., *They Knew The Prophet* (Salt Lake City: Bookcraft Publishers, 1974), 49.

Chapter Three: THE "WHY" OF POLYGAMY

Monogamous wives bore more children than polygamous wives:
"Plural Marriage and Families in Early Utah," n6, Gospel Topics
essay, LDS Church website, n.d., accessed March 11, 2015,
https://www.lds.org/topics/plural-marriage-and-families-in-early-utah?lang=eng.

Comparison of survival rates of children in nineteenth-century Mormondom:
Joseph Henrich, Robert Boyd, Peter J. Richerson, "The puzzle
of monogamous marriage, *Philosophical Transactions of the
Royal Society B: Biological Sciences*, (March 5, 2012), accessed
November 29, 2016, http://www.ncbi.nlm.nih.gov/pmc/articles/
PMC3260845/.

Always more men than women in nineteenth-century Mormondom:
John A. Widstoe, *Evidences and Reconciliations* (Salt Lake City: Bookcraft, 1960), 390.

Polygamy developed from the concept of slavery:
Gerda Lerner, *The Creation of Patriarchy* (New York: Oxford University Press, 1986), 95.

"Polygamy and concubinage wove a thread of disaster":
Elizabeth Cady Stanton, *The Woman's Bible* (Seattle: Coalition Task Force on Women and Religion, 1974), 57.

Mosiah Hancock vision:
Duane Crowther, *Life Everlasting* (Bountiful, Utah: Horizon Publishers, 1997), 96.

Brigham Young on the societal ills of monogamy:
Watt, G.D. et al., eds. (1854–1886). *Journal of Discourses* (London: Latter-Day Saints' Book Depot), 11:128.

Sarah Pea Rich: "a higher glory in the Eternal World":
John Henry Evans, *Charles Coulson Rich: Pioneer Builder of the West* (New York: The Macmillan Company, 1936), 109.

William Clayton: most important doctrine:
Andrew Jenson, *Historical Record*, 1886–1890 (Salt Lake City: Deseret News), 6, 225–27.

B.H. Roberts: "a divinely ordered species of eugenics":
John W. Welch, ed., *The Truth, the Way, the Life: An Elementary Treatise in Theology* (Provo, Utah: Brigham Young University Press, 1996), 556–57.

Polygamy is disadvantageous to students' success:
Adesehinwa Olayinka Adenike, "Effects of family type (monogamy or polygamy) on students' academic achievement in Nigeria," *International Journal of Psychology and Counseling* 5, no.7 (October 2013) 153–56.

Polygamy may contribute to a young man turning to violence:
   Nicholas D. Kristof and Sherry Wudunn, *Half the Sky* (New
   York: Alfred A. Knopf, 2009), 158.

Health hazard of fertile older males:
   James F. Crow, "The high spontaneous mutation rate: Is it a
   health risk?" *Proceedings of the National Academy of Sciences of the
   United States of America* 94, no. 16 (August 1997), accessed July
   7, 2015, http://www.pnas.org/content/94/16/8380.full.

Rare genetic disease in fundamentalist community:
   John Hollenhorst, "Birth defect is plaguing children in FLDS
   town," *Deseret News* (February 9, 2006).

Polygamy undermines social freedom and democracy:
   Stanley Kurtz, "Polygamy vs. Democracy," *The Weekly Standard*
   11, no. 36 (June 5, 2006).

United Nations Human Rights Committee:
   United Nations, "International Covenant on Civil and Political
   Rights," (General Comment No. 28: Equality of rights between
   men and women, article 3), March 29, 2000, accessed September
   9, 2014, http://www1.umn.edu/humanrts/gencomm/hrcom28.
   htm.

Hudson on Canada ruling against polygamy:
   Soraya Chemaly, "What Does Sex Have to Do with World
   Peace?" *Ms.* [blog], November 1, 2012, http://msmagazine.
   com/blog/2012/11/01/what-does-sex-have-to-do-with-world-
   peace/.

Polygamy kept the church in the limelight:
   Brigham H. Roberts, *A Comprehensive History of the Church of
   Jesus Christ of Latter-day Saints* (Salt Lake City: Church of Jesus
   Christ of Latter-day Saints, 1930), 6:227–28.

"Let us be known as a people who love God":
Deiter F. Uchtdorf, "The Love of God," *Ensign* (November 2009), 24.

Polygamy sifted the wheat from the chaff:
Bruce R. McConkie, *Doctrinal New Testament Commentary*, Vol. 1 (Salt Lake City: Deseret Book Company, 2012), 362.

"What is the most shocking thing you have found in the archives?":
James Clayton, interview by Gregory Prince (August 8, 2008), author's private collection.

Young men adopted into Mormon families, young women sealed as wives:
Leonard J. Arrington, *Diary*, (August 4, 1972), author's private collection.

"Fanny, Brother Joseph the Prophet loves you and wishes you for a wife":
Brian C. Hales, "Fanny Alger," *Joseph Smith's Polygamy* [blog], accessed January 23, 2016, http://josephsmithspolygamy.org/plural-wives-overview/fanny-alger/.

Errors of prophets in Old Testament:
Lowell L. Bennion, *Understanding the Scriptures* (Salt Lake City: Deseret Book Company, 1981) 52, 53.

Joseph "did not lust for women so much as he lusted for kin":
Richard Lyman Bushman, *Joseph Smith: Rough Stone Rolling* (New York, Alfred A. Knopf, 2005), 422, 440.

Eliza R. Snow victim of sexual violence:
Peggy Fletcher Stack, "Shocking historical finding: Mormon icon Eliza R. Snow was gang-raped by Missouri ruffians," *Salt Lake Tribune*, March 3, 2016. Available at: http://www.sltrib.com/home/3613791-155/shocking-historical-finding-mormon-icon-eliza.

"With the breath of kindness blow the rest away":
  Dinah Maria Craik, *A Life for a Life,* Volume II (London: Hurst and Brackett, 1859), 84, https://archive.org/details/lifeforlife02crai.

Chapter Four—I WILL TELL EMMA

Going to hell to find Emma:
  Brigham Young, cited in Watt, et al, *Journal of Discourses,* 17:159.

Chapter Five—IS THERE NO HELP FOR THE WIDOW?

Joseph's widows married to other church leaders:
  Todd Compton, *In Sacred Loneliness: The Plural Wives of Joseph Smith* (Salt Lake City: Signature Books, 1997), 83.

Lucy Walker Smith's contract with Heber C. Kimball:
  Ibid., 467.

Chapter Six—THE CELESTIAL LAW

Mary Ann Angell Young: "God will be very cruel":
  Richard S. Van Wagoner, *Mormon Polygamy: A History* (Salt Lake City: Signature Books, 1989), 100.

Brigham Young as kingdom builder:
  Leonard J. Arrington, *Brigham Young: American Moses* (Chicago: University of Illinois Press, 1985), xiii.

"If I were placed on a cannibal island":
  Harold I. Hansen, *A History and Influence of the Mormon Theatre from 1839–1869* (Provo, Utah: Brigham Young University, 1967), iii.

Orson Pratt on the necessity of plural wives:
"A discourse delivered by Elder Orson Pratt, in the Tabernacle, Great Salt Lake City, August 29, 1852," in Watt, et al, *Journal of Discourses,* 1:58.

Hannah Tapfield King: "Did this come from God?":
Rebecca Bartholomew, *Audacious Women: Early British Mormon Immigrants* (Salt Lake City: Signature Books, 1995), 126.

"When properly carried out—on a shovel":
Van Wagoner, *Mormon Polygamy,* 94.

"Might as well deny 'Mormonism'":
"A discourse delivered by Elder Heber C. Kimball, in the Bowery, Great Salt Lake City, October 12, 1856," in Watt, et al, *Journal of Discourses,* 5:203.

Brigham Young on women whining:
"A discourse delivered by President Brigham Young, in the Tabernacle, Great Salt Lake City, September 21, 1856," in Watt, et al, *Journal of Discourses,* 4:55–57.

Women's public vs. private feelings on polygamy:
Arrington, *Diary,* (29 June, 1975), author's private collection.

Phebe Woodruff's personal grief:
Van Wagoner, 101.

Letter from entire church leadership on essential nature of polygamy:
"Proceedings before the Committee on Privileges and Elections of the United States Senate in the Matter of the Protests Against the Right of Hon. Reed Smoot, a Senator from the State of Utah, to Hold His Seat," Vol. II (Washington: Government Printing Office, January 16, 1904–April 13, 1906), 489, accessed December 4, 2015, https://archive.org/details/proceedingsbefo01elecgoog.

Percentage of population in Utah in polygamous families in 1857:
"Plural Marriage and Families in Early Utah," Gospel Topics essay, LDS Church website, n.d., accessed November 7, 2014, https://www.lds.org/topics/plural-marriage-and-families-in-early-utah?lang=eng.

Grew up thinking not as blessed as those having polygamous ancestors:
Andrea Moore-Emmett, *God's Brothel* (San Francisco: Pince-Nez Press, 2004), 14.

Chapter Seven—NO WIFE AT ALL

"He shall find himself in possession of no wife at all":
Brigham Young, "Discourse by President Brigham Young, delivered in the Bowery, at Paris, Oneida County, Idaho, August 31, 1873," in Watt, et al, *Journal of Discourses,* 16:22.

Chapter Eight—OUR MOTHERS WHO ARE IN HEAVEN

"Spirit hands are on my head":
Carol Lynn Pearson, *Beginnings and Beyond* (Springville, Utah: Cedar Fort Inc., 2011), 191.

Joseph Smith on the existence of a Heavenly Mother:
Compton, *In Sacred Loneliness,* 78.

Eliza R. Snow's poem/prayer to the eternal Father and Mother:
Eliza R. Snow, *Poems, Religious, Historical, and Political,* Vol. 1 (Liverpool, 1856), 1–2.

Church News on ancient goddess worship cover-up:
"Scholars expose a 'cover-up,'" *Church News,* October 30, 1983, 7.

Sixteen women in search of God the Mother:
Carol Lynn Pearson, *Mother Wove the Morning* (Walnut Creek, California: Pearson Publishing, 1992).

Many wives needed to people a world:
Orson Pratt, *The Seer*, March 1853, 39. Available at: http://www.
freewebs.com/iglesiadejesucristodeltiempodelfin/Orson Pratt -
The Seer (1854).pdf.

One of the Queens of Heaven:
John Taylor, "Origin, Object, and Destiny of Women,"
The Mormon, August 23, 1857. Available at: http://www.
legrandlbaker.org/wp-content/uploads/2012/10/Taylor-John-
Origin-Object-and-Destiny-of-Women-and-men-by-John-
Taylor.pdf.

Jesus and his wives:
Brigham Young, in Watt, et al, *Journal of Discourses* 13:309.

"Eternal polygamy turns my Heavenly Mother into a sort of amorphous crowd":
Sarah Bringhurst Familia, "Finding my Heavenly Mother,
Part 3," *Times and Seasons* [blog], Oct. 16, 2012, http://
timesandseasons.org/index.php/2012/10/finding-my-heavenly-
mother-part-3-eternal-polygamy-edition/.

Our need for the divine woman:
Raphael Patai, *The Hebrew Goddess* (New York: Avon Books,
1978), 9.

"The more than usually miserable state of the world":
Robert Graves, *The White Goddess* (New York: Farrar, Straus and
Giroux, 1948), 390–91.

"If there is to be a future, it will wear the crown of feminine design":
Andrew Harvey, *The Return of the Mother* (Berkeley: Frog, Ltd.,
1995), xiii, xiv, 1.

Chapter Nine: "HOW DO I LOVE THEE?"

Need for linkages to persons who were essentially assured of exaltation:
Arrington, *Diary*, August 4, 1972, author's private collection.

Lucy Walker: "Place myself upon the altar":
Compton, 464.

Helen Mar Kimball: "My father had but one Ewe Lamb":
Ibid., 498.

Joseph requires Heber C. Kimball to turn over to him his wife Vilate:
Orson F. Whitney, *Life of Heber C. Kimball* (Salt Lake
City: Bookcraft, 1945), 324. Available at: http://
josephsmithspolygamy.org/history/changes-in-february-1842/.

Brigham Young: "Leave them without shedding a tear":
Kathryn M. Daynes, *More Wives than One* (Chicago: University
of Illinois Press, 2001), 64.

Emeline B. Wells: "O, if my husband could only love me even a little":
Van Wagoner, 94.

Romantic love is one of the great possibilities of our existence:
Nathaniel Branden, *The Psychology of Romantic Love* (Los
Angeles: J.P Tarcher, Inc., 1980), 13, 33, 57, 63, 84, 178.

A condition of true romantic love is equality:
Ibid., 24.

Chapter Ten—FIVE PENNIES MAKE A NICKEL, AND WOMEN ARE THE PENNIES

"Freedom's daughters rouse from slumber":
Lula Green Richards, "Woman Arise," in *Utah Woman Suffrage
Songbook* (Salt Lake City, 1871), 5. Available at: https://archive.
org/details/utahwomansuffrag00woma.

Hugh Nibley: patriarchy and matriarchy are both perversions:
Hugh Nibley, "Patriarchy and Matriarchy," (address
given February 1, 1980 to annual women's conference
at Brigham Young University), accessed October 15,
2014, http://publications. maxwellinstitute.byu.edu/
fullscreen/?pub=1065&index=1.

Ancient equalitarian societies:
Riane Eisler, *The Chalice and the Blade* (San Francisco: Harper &
Row, 1987), 31.

Carl Sagan on women free from testosterone poisoning:
Carl Sagan, quotation on back cover of *Women on War* by
Daniella Gioseffi (New York: Feminist Press at City University
of New York, 2003).

In patriarchy whatever men do is seen to have greater value:
Allan G. Johnson, *The Gender Knot: Unraveling Our Patriarchal
Legacy* (Philadelphia: Temple University Press, 1997), 5–9.

Women voters punished as criminals:
Women's Exponent 2 (June 1, 1875), 1.

Susan B. Anthony "humanity's uncrowned queen":
Susa Young Gates and Ann M. Cannon, "Resolutions of
Respect to the Memory of Susan B. Anthony," *Young Woman's
Journal* 17 (May 1906), 208.

Martha Hughes Cannon first female state senator in nation:
Leonard J. Arrington, "Blessed Damozels: Women in Mormon
History," *Dialogue: a Journal of Mormon Thought* 6, no. 2,
(Summer 1971), 30.

"Most remarkable group of women doctors in American history":
Ibid., 27.

Compare women lawyers in Salt Lake City and Santa Cruz:
Woman's Exponent 1 (October 15, 1872), 73–74.

Relief Society wheat donated to San Francisco earthquake survivors in 1906:
Jill Mulvay Derr, Janath Russell Cannon, and Maureen Ursenbach Beecher, *Women of Covenant: The Story of Relief Society* (Salt Lake City: Deseret Book Company, 1992), 72.

One day we may see a woman president of the United States:
Annie Wells Cannon, "Happenings," *Relief Society Magazine* 20 (June 1933), 357.

Relief Society wheat given over to brethren:
Derr, et al., *Women of Covenant*, 335.

Becky Douglas's work with lepers in India:
"Rising Star Outreach," accessed May 12, 2016, http://risingstaroutreach.org/.

Armand Mauss: Correlation brought reduction in power of women:
Peggy Fletcher Stack, "What challenges will the Mormon church face in its 3rd century?", *Salt Lake Tribune*, April 19, 2015. Available at: http://www.sltrib.com/lifestyle/faith/2412535-155/what-challenges-will-mormon-church-face.

Net loss of responsibility and opportunity for women:
Claudia Bushman, "Living and Writing History," *Exponent II*, 34 (2015), 9.

Cannot sit in the corner of a round room:
Eisler, "The Gaia Tradition and the Partnership Future," in *The Chalice and the Blade*, accessed October 21, 2014, http://www.hermes-press.com/CCC/eisler4.htm.

The miracle of Rwanda:
Kristof and Wudunn, *Half the Sky*, 211–12.

Chapter Eleven—TOWARD A PARTNERSHIP FUTURE

Darkness gives way before light:
Joseph Smith, Letter to Oliver Cowdery, Kirtland, Ohio, *Evening and Morning Star*, September 1834, 192. Available at: https://www.lds.org/manual/teachings-joseph-smith/chapter-22?lang=eng.

Mistreatment of women globally:
Jimmy Carter, "Why I believe the mistreatment of women is the number one human rights abuse," TED talk, given May, 2015, http://www.ted.com/talks/jimmy_carter_why_i_believe_the_mistreatment_of_women_is_the_number_one_human_rights_abuse.

President McKay sometimes allowed women to be sealed to more than one husband:
Hugh B. Brown, *An Abundant Life* (Salt Lake City: Signature Books, 1988), 121.

Hymn changed to eliminate "red men" and "rude delights":
P. Jane Hafen, "'Great Spirit Listen:' The American Indian in Mormon Music," *Dialogue: A Journal of Mormon Thought* 18, no.4 (Winter 1985), 133. Available at: http://www.dialoguejournal.com/wp-content/uploads/sbi/articles/Dialogue_V18N04_135.pdf.

Various changes made in lyrics of hymnal and hopes for future:
Douglas Campbell, "Changes in LDS Hymns: Implications and Opportunities," *Dialogue: A Journal of Mormon Thought* 28, no.3 (Fall 1995), 66, 72, 79, 91. Available at: https://www.dialoguejournal.com/wp-content/uploads/sbi/articles/Dialogue_V28N03_79.pdf.

Pure and delightsome or white and delightsome:
John A. Tvedtnes, "The Charge of 'Racism' in the Book of Mormon," FairMormon Conference, 2003, accessed February 11, 2015, http://www.fairmormon.org/perspectives/fair-conferences/2003-fair-conference/2003-the-charge-of-racism-in-the-book-of-mormon.

Racial references in Book of Mormon headings:
Peggy Fletcher Stack, "Church removes racial references in Book of Mormon," *Salt Lake Tribune*, December 20, 2010. Available at: http://archive.sltrib.com/story.php?ref=/sltrib/home/50882900-76/mormon-book-changes-church.html.csp.

Leaders have made mistakes:
Deiter F. Uchtdorf, "Come, Join With Us," *Ensign* (November 2013), 22, http://media.ldscdn.org/pdf/magazines/ensign-november-2013/2013-11-08-come-join-with-us-eng.pdf.

Mormons have never believed in inerrant prophets or inerrant scripture:
"Doctrine and Covenants/Textual changes," FairMormon Answers, accessed August 17, 2015, http://en.fairmormon.org/Doctrine_and_Covenants/Textual_changes/Why_did_Joseph_Smith_edit_revelations.

Section 132 dropped from Doctrine and Covenants by James E. Talmage:
James P. Harris, *Latter-day Revelation: Selections from the Book of Doctrine and Covenants Containing Revelations Given through Joseph Smith the Prophet* (Salt Lake City: Signature Books, 2003), xxviii, xxix, xxxii.

Law of adoption an incorrect procedure:
FairMormon Answers, accessed August 17, 2015, http://en.fairmormon.org/Mormonism_and_polygamy/The_Law_of_Adoption.

Removal of priesthood ban for black men:
Edward L. Kimball, "Spencer W. Kimball and the Revelation on Priesthood," *BYU Studies* 47, no. 2 (2008), 4–78, https://ojs.lib.byu.edu/spc/index.php/BYUStudies/article/viewFile/7325/6974.

Disavowal of all racism in LDS history and present:
"Race and the Priesthood," The Church of Jesus Christ of Latter-day Saints, 2013, Gospel Topics essay, LDS Church website, n.d., accessed November 2, 2015, https://www.lds.org/topics/race-and-the-priesthood?lang=eng.

Richard Bushman, "drains the ban of revelatory significance":
Peggy Fletcher Stack, "Mormon church traces black priesthood ban to Brigham Young," *Salt Lake Tribune*, December 16, 2013. Available at: http://archive.sltrib.com/story.php?ref=/sltrib/news/57241071-78/church-priesthood-black-smith.html.csp.

Gordon B. Hinckley on church giving up polygamy long ago:
Gordon B. Hinckley, interview by Larry King, *Larry King Live*, CNN, September 8, 1998, transcript, accessed October 20, 2014, http://www.lds-mormon.com/lkl_00.shtml.

President Kimball on fighting his own assumptions about race:
Church News, January 6, 1979, 4.

About the Author

Carol Lynn Pearson is the author of more than 40 books and plays that together have sold over 800,000 copies—autobiography, inspiration, humor, and novellas. She claims to have been "born into women's issues" and "married into gay issues," both of which she has fearlessly addressed on the difficult terrain of religion.

She considers her newest book, *The Ghost of Eternal Polygamy,* to be one of the most important works of her literary career and a vital move forward in the worldwide tide toward transforming Patriarchy into Partnership.

Ms. Pearson was born in Salt Lake City, received an M.A. in theatre from Brigham Young University, and lives in Walnut Creek, California. Visit her at:

carollynnpearson.com
facebook.com/clpauthor

On her website is a repository for stories like the ones you have read in this book. If you have a personal story to share, you are invited to do so.

Made in United States
Troutdale, OR
10/14/2024

23725623R00148